797,885 Books

are available to read at

Forgotten Books

www.ForgottenBooks.com

Forgotten Books' App
Available for mobile, tablet & eReader

ISBN 978-1-331-13628-6
PIBN 10149111

This book is a reproduction of an important historical work. Forgotten Books uses state-of-the-art technology to digitally reconstruct the work, preserving the original format whilst repairing imperfections present in the aged copy. In rare cases, an imperfection in the original, such as a blemish or missing page, may be replicated in our edition. We do, however, repair the vast majority of imperfections successfully; any imperfections that remain are intentionally left to preserve the state of such historical works.

Forgotten Books is a registered trademark of FB &c Ltd.
Copyright © 2017 FB &c Ltd.
FB &c Ltd, Dalton House, 60 Windsor Avenue, London, SW19 2RR.
Company number 08720141. Registered in England and Wales.

For support please visit www.forgottenbooks.com

1 MONTH OF FREE READING

at
www.ForgottenBooks.com

By purchasing this book you are eligible for one month membership to ForgottenBooks.com, giving you unlimited access to our entire collection of over 700,000 titles via our web site and mobile apps.

To claim your free month visit:
www.forgottenbooks.com/free149111

* Offer is valid for 45 days from date of purchase. Terms and conditions apply.

English
Français
Deutsche
Italiano
Español
Português

www.forgottenbooks.com

Mythology Photography **Fiction** Fishing Christianity **Art** Cooking Essays **Buddhism** Freemasonry Medicine **Biology** Music **Ancient Egypt** Evolution Carpentry Physics Dance Geology **Mathematics** Fitness Shakespeare **Folklore** Yoga Marketing **Confidence** Immortality Biographies Poetry **Psychology** Witchcraft Electronics Chemistry History **Law** Accounting **Philosophy** Anthropology Alchemy Drama Quantum Mechanics Atheism Sexual Health **Ancient History Entrepreneurship** Languages Sport Paleontology Needlework Islam **Metaphysics** Investment Archaeology Parenting Statistics Criminology **Motivational**

DEPARTMENT OF EDUCATION
THE CITY OF NEW YORK

SIXTEENTH ANNUAL REPORT

OF THE

CITY SUPERINTENDENT OF SCHOOLS

1913–1914

REPORTS ON DEFECTIVE CHILDREN

    MENTAL DEFECTIVES
    THE ANAEMIC
    THE TUBERCULOUS
    THE BLIND
    THE DEAF AND DUMB
    THE CRIPPLED
    VISITING TEACHERS

PRESENTED TO THE BOARD OF EDUCATION
DECEMBER 9, 1914

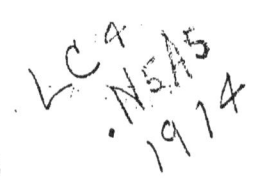

TABLE OF CONTENTS

	PAGE
LETTER OF TRANSMITTAL..	4
REPORT ON UNGRADED (MENTALLY ATYPICAL) CLASSES...............	7–31
Advisory Council..	7
Type of medical examination.....................................	8–9
Segregation of types of atypical children........................	10
Existing administrative staff inadequate........................	11–15
Difficulty in establishing ungraded classes.....................	16
Number and distribution of ungraded classes and register of pupils..	16
Schools proposing children for ungraded classes.................	17
Insufficient clerical staff.......................................	18–19
Laboratory...	19
Visiting teachers...	19–20
Visiting teachers' report of work................................	21–27
Survey of results of ungraded class training....................	28–31
Summary of recommendations..................................	31
REPORT ON OPEN-AIR CLASSES......................................	32–54
Classes for tuberculous children................................	32–33
Advantages of schooling for tuberculous children...............	33–34
Effect of cold air on tuberculous children.......................	34–35
Statistics..	36
Schools having anæmic classes..................................	37
Temperature of classrooms.....................................	38
Kind and situation of open-air classrooms......................	38–39
Proper equipments of rooms and clothing of children...........	39–40
Results of these classes on physical condition...................	40–41
Permanency of results...	41–42
Need for more anæmic classes...................................	42
Statistics..	43–45
Open-window classes for normal children.......................	46–48
Teachers' reports on such classes...............................	48–49
Suggestions for management of open-window classes............	50–53
Problems of ventilation...	53–54

	PAGE
CLASSES FOR BLIND CHILDREN	55–62
Reference to death of Miss Gertrude E. Bingham	55
Statistics	55–56
Classes in elementary schools	56
Pupils in high schools	56–58
Work in printing office for the blind	58
Vocational training in connection with blind pupils in our classes	58–60
Physical training—Athletics	60
Lectures for blind children in American Museum of Natural History	62
Eye examinations at clinic	62
Glasses for children with defective vision	62
SCHOOL FOR THE DEAF	63–71
Statistics	63–64
Origin and distribution of deafness	64–66
Physical care of the deaf	66–68
The mental side	68–69
Industrial work for the deaf	69–70
The graduates of the school	70–71
Need of a new building	71
The voice	71
CLASSES FOR CRIPPLED CHILDREN	73–75
Statistics	73
East Side Free School Association for Crippled Children	74
Association for the Aid of Crippled Children	74
Industrial work	74
Proposed inspection of classes for crippled children	75
REPORT ON VISITING TEACHERS	78–84
General purpose and method of work	78
Summary of cases treated	79
Conditions investigated	79
Conditions found	79
Action taken	79
Outcome of investigation	80
Agencies that co-operated with the visiting teachers	80
A few significant cases	80–81
Testimony of principals	81–84
Testimony of district superintendents	84

LETTER OF TRANSMITTAL.

NEW YORK, July 20, 1914.

TO THE BOARD OF EDUCATION:

Ladies and Gentlemen:

I have the honor to present in this pamphlet the reports of our school work for defective children—the mentally defective, the anemic, the tuberculous, the blind, the deaf and dumb, and the crippled.

A feature of the report prepared by Miss Elizabeth E. Farrell, Inspector of Ungraded Classes (classes for mentally defective children), is the account of the work of two visiting teachers, appointed for the first time last year. Another interesting feature is a survey of the after life of 86 atypical boys and 38 atypical girls who left the ungraded classes after a training of three or four years. The survey shows that 54 per cent of these children are now engaged in some kind of remunerative employment.

Miss Farrell shows very clearly the necessity for more laboratory and office space to conduct the examination of children alleged to be mentally defective, of more physicians to examine them, of more visiting teachers to discover life histories and to bring the home into co-operation with the school, of more trained teachers to train these unfortunate children when they are gathered into classrooms, and of more classrooms in which to grade them in accordance with the degree of defect.

Dr. I. Ogden Woodruff, who for three years, without remuneration, inspected and reported upon open-air classes, became, during the year, a salaried officer of the Board of Education, with special assignment to the supervision of all open-air classes. His report will be found valuable, not only because of his clear account of what was accomplished during the year in our three kinds of open-air classes—classes for the tuberculous, classes for the anæmic, which care for children who are subnormal physically, and open-window classes for normal children,—but more particularly for his demonstration of the permanence of the good effects produced by open-air classes and his suggestions to principals and teachers for the management of open-window classes for normal pupils. A study of this report would scarcely fail to impress your Board with the propriety—if not the necessity—of largely increasing the facilities for teaching in the open air.

The Report on Classes for the Blind shows that substantial progress is being made in the work of teaching the blind. The suggestion that a special teacher of music, to train blind children endowed with the musical gift, be appointed, is worthy of careful consideration.

The need of a new building in which to carry on the beneficent work of teaching the deaf to speak and to understand what others say by reading their lips, and to provide increased opportunity for vocational training, is ably set forth by Miss Carrie W. Kearns, Principal of the School for the Deaf.

Superintendent Edson, who reports on the classes for crippled children, shows the necessity of gathering these classes into centrally located and specially equipped buildings.

Because of the intimate connection between the work of visiting teachers and the school work of mentally and physically defective children (though the work of the visiting teacher is not by any means limited to such children), I publish in this pamphlet Superintendent Edson's account of the work accomplished by visiting teachers.

Eight visiting teachers were appointed during the year. Their work has been carefully watched. Mr. Edson's report is extremely valuable, because of its summary of the testimony to the worth of this work borne by district superintendents and principals. I sincerely trust that this testimony will lead to a very great enlargement of the corps of visiting teachers. In a small city or village, where the population is fairly homogeneous, where all teachers live near their work, and where the schools are not crowded, necessary visiting at homes may be done by the regular staff of teachers. Such is not the case, however, in a city of the dimensions of New York, or even a city much smaller. In a community in which teachers frequently live at a great distance from their schools, in which the teacher, at the close of the day's work is worn out by the management of crowded classes, and in which a very large proportion of the parents do not speak English, the work of visiting homes becomes a special function. Many of our principals and teachers, particularly the kindergarten teachers, do much visiting at homes. Nor should this work be discontinued. The conscientious teacher will always find work of this kind to do. But there are so many cases in which, in order to bring about due correlation between the work of the school and the work of the home, so much time and so much energy and so much sympathy are required, that the class teacher cannot possibly bring about the desired results. Her reserves of time, energy, and sympathy are not sufficient. For such cases the visiting teacher becomes a necessity.

I urgently recommend that the force of visiting teachers be increased from eight to twenty-five.

Respectfully yours,

WM. H. MAXWELL,
City Superintendent of Schools

MENTAL DEFECTIVES

Report on Work of Ungraded Classes

(From Report of Miss Elizabeth E. Farrell, Inspector of Ungraded Classes)

ADVISORY COUNCIL

The most significant thing in the history of the ungraded class movement in New York City is the acceptance during the last year by the Department of Education of the services of public-spirited men and women to serve in the capacity of advisers to the Department of Ungraded Classes. In offering their services to the city, the Council set forth as its objects:

1.—To work out a type of examination for children who are backward in their school work.

2.—To formulate public opinion with regard to adequate institutional provision for such children as need it.

3.—To recommend such legal protection for children entering industry from ungraded classes as seems desirable.

4.—To advise with regard to types and methods of training for atypical children in the public schools.

The Advisory Council is made up of experienced alienists, neurologists, educators, sociologists, and psychologists, as follows:

L. Pierce Clark, M.D.	Mrs. Wesley C. Mitchell
Charles L. Dana, M.D.	Frederick Peterson, M.D.
Stephen Pierce Duggan, Ph.D.	James Putnam, M.D.
August Hoch, M.D.	Bernard Sachs, M.D.
Eleanor Hope Johnson	Israel Strauss, M.D.
Mrs. Florence Kelley	Lillian D. Wald
Foster Kennedy, M.D.	Elizabeth E. Farrell, Secretary
Adolf Meyer, M.D.	

Their conspicuous contribution to the work in the schools during the past year has been twofold. In conference with the regular staff, a type of examination has been worked out which is in accord with the best traditions in this work. They have taken an aggressive part in initiating legislation affecting the mentally deficient throughout the State. They have advocated publicly and privately the passage of a bill giving the Governor authority to appoint a Commission of five persons to investigate present provision for the care of the mentally deficient in this State and to outline a program for its improvement.

TYPE OF MEDICAL EXAMINATION

The type of medical examination was worked out after certain neurologists of the Advisory Council had given at least one afternoon a week in this office for the purpose of seeing certain selected cases referred by the examiners on the regular staff. Attention should be given to the detail which characterizes these examinations. We are not satisfied with examination by one person, with the results of one test, such as the Binet-Simon test, but each case is studied and tested by different individuals. In every difficult case as many as four examiners try to analyze the mind not only on its intellectual side but on the emotional and on the volitional as well. To understand a case thoroughly we must not rely entirely upon laboratory tests. They must be supplemented by records of social and economic efficiency. This necessitates, therefore, the consideration of the following groups of data: 1—Record of school achievement; 2—Record of home and environmental conditions; 3—Record of neurological and psychological examination; 4—Record of personality study.

TYPE OF EXAMINATION AND RECORD

CASE I. The study is based upon a boy, aged fourteen years, who is totally unable to make any progress in the ordinary book work of his school. He cannot spell the simplest words, such as "girl" or "desk," and does not know the three times table in multiplication. His sense training in the school is but fair. He was especially quick to respond to commands in all physical training. His handwriting was shaky and much of his industrial training was accompanied by trembling movements. He speaks well. His reading and arithmetic are equal to a boy's of seven years. The amount of general information is fair. His power of attention and memory is good. In the ungraded class he does good manual labor.

The family history is negative, and throws no light on the causes of his mental defect. An inquiry into the personal history is negative aside from an attack of scarlet fever at three years of age. A year after the fever, which was moderately severe, he had two or three peculiar faint turns which pointed to a certain type of epileptic fits, but nothing similar to them has occurred since. He is a robust, fine looking, bright boy, with no apparent physical or nervous disorder.

Careful test shows his intellectual development to be that of a boy of seven years. He stands in great terror of his father and the teachers, who think he is lazy and unwilling to learn. At home, he reads his lessons over and over again before the father comes home at night so that the father will not hear his mistakes and scold him, but he continues to make mistakes in spite of all efforts. The main examination shows that he has a good disposition. He went through all the manual and motor tests easily and well. It was found that ever since the attack of scarlet fever at three years, he has been sluggish and indifferent to any kind of work requiring visual memory. He has always been poorest in spelling. His motor cleverness and ability to handle and understand mechanical work is well shown in an incident of last summer, while in the country on a vacation. He wanted to take two broken bicycles apart and make one good one out of the remnants; after days of labor and constructive adaptation he succeeded in accomplishing the task, in spite of receiving advice that it could not be done. It is found that he has gradually become a timid type of boy who never plays freely or naturally with other children and always prefers to be alone. He is interested in electrical work and attends to the electric bells in his home, and in fact does all the repair jobs about the house. He is employed by the teachers in his school at all sorts of work. His very lack of getting on at school seems to have engendered a shyness, timidity, and feeling of inadequacy and doubt, which in turn are slowly shutting him out of daily friendly contact with the outside world. He is becoming morose and solitary in habits. What the boy himself has to say is as follows:

"I don't know why I can't get on at school; I can't spell nor write nor do arithmetic. I can do any sort of hand work; I seem to understand that by nature, but I can't carry anything in my mind. I mean I can't see a thing in the shop window and go home and make any part of the toy or machine by having just seen it in the shop. I want to be an electrician, but realize I must know more about books if I am to do any good work in life. If I could get an education through my hands it would be easy."

SEGREGATION OF TYPES OF ATYPICAL CHILDREN

It will not be understood that an examination such as that detailed above is given to every child who is proposed for an ungraded class. The obvious case of mental defect is easy to detect. The borderline cases, the nervous children, in which group are found those afflicted with hysteria, habit spasms, fears, epilepsies, the timid, shy, depressed, the excitable types, the delinquent and the truant, call for all phases of physical and mental testing in order that their reactions and the depth and breadth of their personalities may be somewhat laid bare.

The children in this second group present some of the most serious problems in community life. On every hand researches are being made into the causes of vagrancy, crime, pauperism and the diseases of social life, but in all of these researches it is a product, a result that is dealt with. The research student in penology, like the alienist, must view in retrospect the individual's life, and reconstruct, if possible, the early youth and childhood of the person who is a pauper, a criminal, or a mental wreck. Even if it were possible to reconstruct accurately the past of these unfortunate individuals, the greatest difficulty is still ahead of the worker. A cure, a reformation is to be effected. This means that the individual must be re-educated, re-formed; his habits and instincts and interests must be re-established and in the right way. To do this in adult life is almost an impossible task. If the tendencies had been detected while the personality was still plastic enough to permit of change, we might have prevented that which it is difficult if not impossible to cure.

Examinations such as have been indicated above have yielded results. It is proposed to individualize ungraded classes, to put into a given class those children whose needs are similar. An endeavor will be made to have teachers informed as to the characteristic phases of the work in these special classes. They will know the children best. They will be encouraged to study the instinctive life of the child as it develops, to analyze the component parts of the individual's personality, to determine the formative traits or trends of character, in order that educational changes or environmental changes may be made as seem necessary.

EXISTING ADMINISTRATIVE STAFF INADEQUATE

The additions to the administrative staff were made in September, 1913. It is to be regretted, however, that the requests granted at that time for additional help were those made some three years ago. They were based on the amount of work turned into this office during 1910–1911. It is needless to say that the acquisitions were entirely inadequate to the amount of work to be done in 1914. Therefore it becomes necessary again to call attention to the fact that additional physicians, inspectors and social workers are urgently needed at once to do the work of the department.

In no place is the inadequacy of our staff so evident as in the conduct of clinics for the examination of children who are not obviously defective. Their examination demands special equipment and apparatus, quiet and time to do the work. It is imperative that more such clinics should be held. Instead of having only two central places of examination, there should be at least one such place in each borough. While the work has been done at four central clinics a week during the past year, it is hoped that we shall be able to devote each afternoon in the week and Saturday morning to the examination of these higher types of variant mentality.

Elementary school principals, the permanent census bureau and child welfare agencies proposed 4,739 children for examination. This is the largest number to be referred in any one year. It seems to confirm what has long been felt that as soon as the number of workers is at all commensurate, the amount of work to be done is increasingly in evidence. Of this number a total of 2,956 were examined. The difference between the number proposed and the number actually examined is very great. It is to be explained, however, by the fact that Dr. Smart has been absent for several months because of serious personal illness.

RE-EXAMINATION

It is again necessary to report that the re-examination of all children in ungraded classes has been impossible. That the regular school grades might not be too seriously burdened by the presence in them of slow and defective children, the policy has been to do the new work whenever possible. The children in the ungraded classes have been neglected. It would be hard to exaggerate the necessity of regular re-examinations of these children. Their improvement is to come, if at all, with improved physical, hygienic, and educational treatment and training.

13

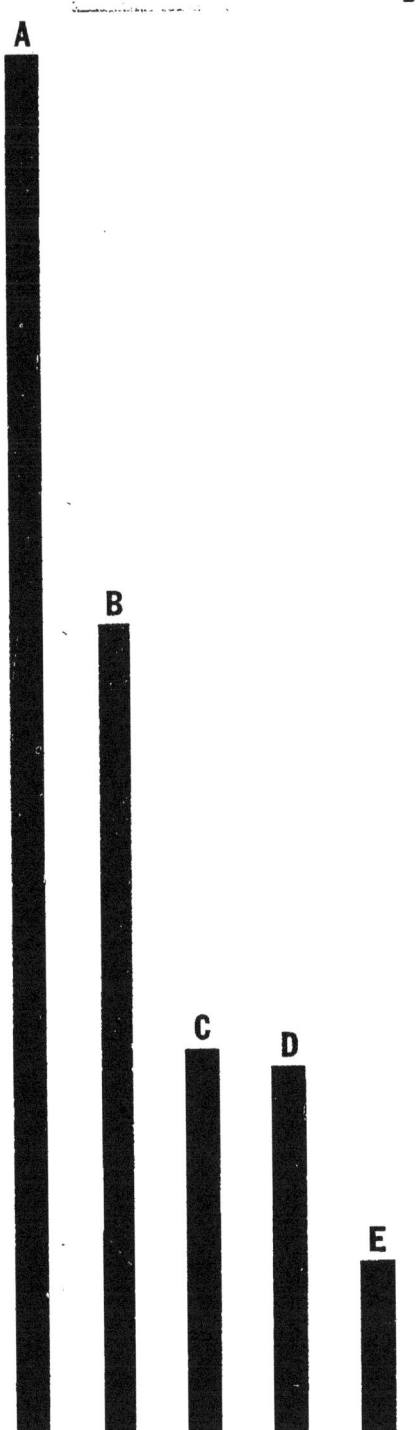

A = No. Cases Reported.
B = " " Examined.
C = " " Not Examined.
D = " " Approved.
E = " " Not Approved.

A { 1.—Medical staff in 1906.
    2.—No children proposed in 1906.

B { 1.—Medical staff in 1914.
    2.—No. children proposed in 1914.

Year	Number Reported	Number Examined	Not Examined.
1912–1913	3430	1791	1639
1913–1914	4739	2956	1783

A[1] = No. Cases Proposed 1912–13.
A[2] = " " Examined 1912–13.
B[1] = " " Proposed 1913–14.
B[2] = " " Examined 1913–14.

DIFFICULTY IN ESTABLISHING UNGRADED CLASSES

In organizing ungraded classes one of the greatest difficulties is in finding a suitable room. In a given month during the spring term just ended, the district superintendents of schools throughout the city reported approximately one thousand children examined and approved for ungraded class work but not in such classes. A similar survey of available rooms in school buildings, or in annexes to the same, evidenced the inability to organize additional classes unless property could be rented for the purpose. It seems desirable to have money set aside for this purpose. I beg to recommend that ten thousand dollars, for the rental of rooms in which ungraded classes may be organized, be included in the school budget for 1915.

NUMBER AND DISTRIBUTION OF UNGRADED CLASSES

To this date 192 ungraded classes have been authorized by the Board of Superintendents. Of this number 184 were in actual operation during the whole or part of the school year just closed. The remaining eight classes will be organized in September, 1914.

The distribution of ungraded classes by boroughs is as follows:

UNGRADED CLASSES
1914

Borough	Classes June 30 after promotion	Additional classes authorized for Sept.	Total classes authorized	Register June 30 1914	Teachers	Vacancies	For classes to be organized
Manhattan...	92	0	92	1,496	67	25	0
The Bronx...	14	4	18	223	13	1	4
Brooklyn....	64	1	65	1,002	43	21	1
Queens......	16	*2	17	201	15	1	1
Richmond...	3	..	3	50	3	..	..
Total......	189	6	195	2,972	141	48	6

*1 class discontinued.

SCHOOLS PROPOSING CHILDREN FOR UNGRADED CLASSES

As has been done in former years, school principals were asked to report children whom they thought to be in need of ungraded class work. This request was made in the following way:

"*To Principals of Elementary Schools,*

    LADIES AND GENTLEMEN:

I am sending you under separate cover application forms for the examination of children whom you propose for ungraded class work. (These children should be brought immediately to the attention of the school doctor and the school nurse for care and treatment.) I suggest that you give your personal attention to the conspicuously backward children; those obviously mentally defective; those three years behind in their school work; those who are apparently unable to learn to read; those who have very deficient number sense; those who are truants; those who seem incorrigible and noticeably irritable and nervous. In judging the above points allowance should be made for the child's lack of educational opportunities.

It is proposed to examine the children in accordance with the following schedule:

SCHEDULE

September, 1913.....................................June, 1914

DISTRICTS

September 6, 8, 13, 14	February
October 1, 2, 11, 16, 23, 25, 32, 37, 41, 43, 45	March
November 4, 7, 15, 18, 19, 24, 28, 34, 39, 46	April
December 3, 9, 10, 12, 20, 26, 27, 33, 36, 38	May
January 5, 17, 21, 22, 29, 30, 31, 35, 40, 42, 44	June

Because of the great pressure of work only such children will be examined as have been reported to this office at least ten days (10 days) prior to the first day of the month indicated for the different districts. It is imperative that the parent or some responsible person be present at the examination, which will be held in a school building to be determined later.

I take pleasure in informing you that clinics for the examination of children are held each week in the Manhattan office on Thursday afternoon and Saturday morning and in the Brooklyn office Tuesday afternoon and Saturday morning. In order that unnecessary hardship to parents may be avoided, it is essential that appointments be made for children who are to be examined.

                Respectfully,

                WILLIAM H. MAXWELL,
                    City Superintendent of Schools."

The response to this letter is as follows:

Number of Elementary Schools	...	505
Number of schools that did report	326	...
Number of schools that did not report	179	...
Total	...	505

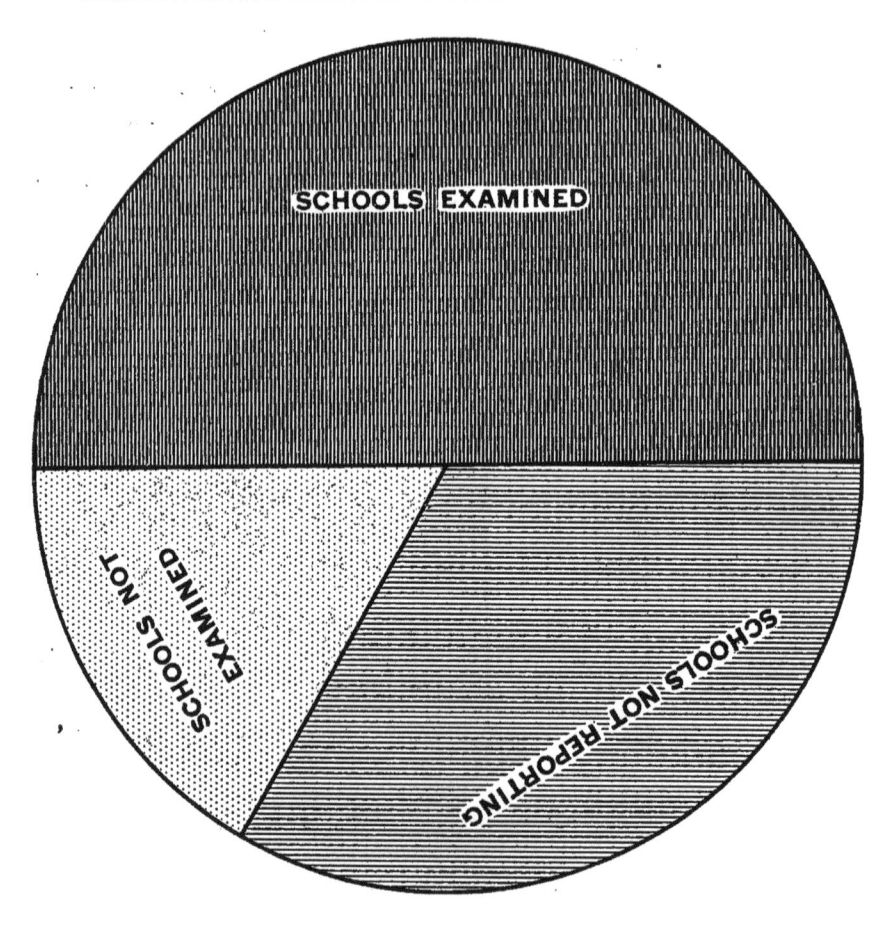

CLERICAL STAFF

The conditions which prevailed last year and which were presented in the last annual report still obtain with regard to the clerical staff. A large part of the work is done by sustitute teachers without any special preparation in office work. This means that they must be trained by their daily work. It also means that the daily work is never accomplished within the day. There is always much more to be done than can possibly be accomplished with the staff as it exists at present.

LABORATORY

It is discouraging to report again that nothing has been done in the matter of providing adequate laboratory room. One of the physicians, as well as the social workers, has been obliged to use any desk which at the time might be unused. He has had no place to call his own, no possible way of taking care of his materials and supplies. Such an arrangement does not make for efficiency. That it should be continued seems incredible.

VISITING TEACHERS

For the first time in the history of any school system in this country, if not in the world, visiting teachers, whose function is that of social workers, have been officially licensed to do for the children what the best teachers in smaller and less complex communities have always done. We have learned that if this service is left undone, it is at a great cost to the children and ultimately to the State. The hospital learned some years ago that its expensive care was made more expensive when recovery was delayed because of certain conditions in the home which caused worry to the sick person; while others in need of convalescent care did not receive it if left to themselves. The consequence was they were often forced to return to the hospital for a more or less prolonged stay. The condition in the school is similar, particularly with those children who are slow and retarded. To know that they need glasses and to do nothing further is to be willing to repeat the expensive work of the school; to bring a slow and retarded child for a physical and mental examination without submitting definite information of his environmental setting and of his family and personal developmental history is to waste the time of several people, deny the child his best opportunity, and by so doing waste public funds. The story of this new factor in public education is told by the visiting teachers, Miss Brown and Miss Culp, in their report of the year's work, which I take pleasure in submitting.

WHERE THEY GO TO

- SCHOOLS
- FRESH AIR CLASSES
- SCHOOLS FOR THE DEAF
- INSTITUTIONS FOR FEEBLE-MINDED
- CONVALESCENT HOMES
- HOSPITALS
- DISPENSARIES
- PHYSICIANS
- DENTAL CLINICS
- DENTISTS
- PHILANTHROPIC SOCIETIES
- EDUCATIONAL SOCIETIES
- SETTLEMENTS
- SOCIETY FOR THE PREVENTION OF CRUELTY TO CHILDREN
- DEPT. OF HEALTH
- DEPT. OF PUBLIC CHARITIES
- DEPT. OF LABOR
- DEPT. OF CORRECTIONS
- DEPT. OF IMMIGRATION
- CHILD LABOR COMMITTEE
- PUBLIC LIBRARIES
- BUSINESS HOUSES
- PRIVATE INDIVIDUALS FOR FRIENDLY VISITING

THE DEPARTMENT OF UNGRADED CLASSES

WHERE THEY COME FROM

- PUBLIC SCHOOLS
- PAROCHIAL SCHOOLS
- CHILDREN'S COURTS
- PERMANENT CENSUS BUREAU
- HOSPITALS
- DISPENSARIES
- PHILANTHROPIC SOCIETIES
- EDUCATIONAL SOCIETIES
- SOCIETY FOR THE PREVENTION OF CRUELTY TO CHILDREN
- SETTLEMENTS
- PHYSICIANS
- PARENTS
- PRIVATE INDIVIDUALS

VISITING TEACHERS' REPORT OF WORK

The work is old, as old as the public schools. At first it was done by the teachers; often with more kindness than judgment, visiting here, teaching there things not written in books, giving often from a slender purse. Later, volunteer visitors from churches and clubs made occasional appearance in school, and sometimes straightened difficulties in the homes. Then, as the philanthropic societies grew up, the principals and teachers came to refer their children to them, and social workers went to the homes from the societies. Then the educational societies took up the work and as need arose have loaned skilled workers year by year to organize and practice a maximum of good with a minimum of confusion; and now the regularly appointed visiting teacher—is she not part of the logical development of the school?

All stages of social service still exist, but unevenly. Visiting teachers have come to fill the gaps where social work is not done, and to relieve those principals, who, possessing the shepherd spirit, know only too well how much time, energy and money are spent in referring, conferring and visiting, and realize that this should be the work of one person with training, skill and time to work for results. Why should the workers be attached to schools? Because we know the children, and we know each child's brothers and sisters, mothers, families—some for months, some for years. Because, though we can co-operate with other organizations, we cannot direct them. "Co-operation" is a great slogan, but it does not mean asking somebody else to do the work.

WE SERVE
1. The children
2. The parents
3. The principals and teachers
4. The Department of Ungraded Classes
5. The Department of Education
6. The co-operating agencies

Each call naturally involves some benefit to all six bodies of people, but the degrees vary in each case. For instance, if the visiting teacher visits the public library to find a list of suitable reading for a high-grade mental defective, the class teacher is not as likely to reap immediate and general satisfaction therefrom as if the visiting teacher were conducting a child with a discharging ear to the dispensary, or urging a careless mother to send her child to school clean; yet all are good visits. In the same way the mother does not see the particular benefit to her in an unexpected call from a stranger who questions her on the subject of convulsions over and done with ten years ago, but the doctor who examines the child does. Then when Jenny knows more history than the teacher thought or when the mother learns that by proper care her boy may escape epileptic attacks, the purpose of our work begins to be appreciated.

Special cases needing adjustment. The adjustment of special cases seems to take up most of our time. For instance, the truants who have to be coaxed in the home or on the street corner day after day; the cases of home guardianship so bad that children disappear for days; the guiding of children to institutions and persuading parents to let them stay. For example: John Kennedy, a low grade defective, was kept home on the (verbal) advice of a doctor who said he has brain tumor and a weak heart. The visiting teacher went to the home and in the course of conversation found that the doctor's treatment consists of very expensive pills and "plenty of fresh air and exercise." The fresh air was acquired on the father's vegetable cart and the exercise consisted of carrying loads of potatoes to the top floors of tenements. Armed with this information the visiting teacher telephoned the doctor, who had seen the boy but twice. Would he advise institutional care? Yes. Did he know the work of the ungraded classes? No. He thought the boy was in a 4B grade. After this conversation the doctor and visiting teacher advised in harmony as follows:

1. Permanent Custodial care, or
2. Ungraded class every day, and
3. No peddling of vegetables under threat of the Child Labor Committee.

Investigation of homes preliminary to the doctor's examination. Children examined in school for the ungraded classes and at the office clinics are not always accompanied by a parent, hence the family history is not available for the doctor's information. Also it is quite true that the mothers are more apt to be truthful and explicit at their own firesides than they are among strangers in the office. It is often necessary to interview members of the family, school teachers, and family physicians before all the information needed for a complete understanding of the child's mental and physical condition can be obtained.

Following up the doctor's recommendations. Home visits are necessary to follow up the examining physician's recommendation. It is necessary to analyze the child's environmental conditions, hereditary influences and temperamental tendencies, as a basis for treatment. For instance, in a case of malnutrition we must find the cause in order to correct it. Is the child's condition due to lack of food, poor food, poor cooking, hasty meals, impaired digestion, too much candy, decayed teeth, or adenoids? In the case of a choreic child, is chorea due to previous illness, fright, cruel or drunken parents, late hours, excitement, over-stimulation by coffee, eye defect? We must know the child and the whole family very well before we can hope to accomplish much. When the school nurses have these same children on their records, we work with them. Only workers who have watched the same children for years know the difficulties of maintaining a standard of good health. As yet we can deal only with the more immediate cases, but as every child examined does not enter an ungraded class, here is a chance for excellent co-operation with the visiting teachers of the Public Education Association. Provided there were somebody to gather in reports from the co-operating visiting teachers, who almost in every instance know the families before the children are proposed for ungraded classes, then the recommendations of the children not admitted to Ungraded Classes, could be returned to the original visiting teacher, while the advice to those admitted could be followed up by the visiting teacher attached to this office.

Following up children discharged from school. We try to trace children who have left ungraded classes, especially those who are discharged at sixteen years. This is work requiring much patience and inspiration. On the desk beside this report lies a letter from the Charity Organization Society promising one more glass eye to Tom Dunn, to equip him for seeking work, and beneath it lies a list of "Boys Wanted," cut out of a newspaper ready to send to another boy's mother.

All of these cases prove the need of constant supervision; and in all our visiting we must be constantly urging the parents to their responsibility toward their mentally defective children. This education of the parents, which is one of the first principles of our work, should be a field for a much wider propaganda. Every child who has left the ungraded class to go to work would probably be working more efficiently and making more money under sympathetic "after care." A sort of continued oversight until their needs are demonstrated and met would help, beyond a doubt.

Following up cases reported by the Census Bureau. Children reported by the permanent census bureau who have not been brought to this office on request must be looked up by the visiting teacher. These are our saddest cases. They do not often prove to be children who would be helped by ungraded class work, but they frequently need institutional and sometimes medical care.

For example: Little Dennis Kelley, the son of a bankrupt saloon keeper, was reported to the office of Classes for the Blind. The visitor from that office reported him to us as a mental defective, and our visiting teacher guessed him a hopeless idiot, nearly blind, with tuberculosis of the knee. While there was money, Dennis had had doctors; when the money went the treatment ceased. The father and mother loving him more than the other five children, kept him at home in three dark rooms. They could not bear to take this little child to the hurried doctors of dispensaries, even if he could have stood the strain of visiting three different clinics. Dennis is now in a beautiful country hospital growing larger and stronger. His parents, devout Catholics, trust him entirely to the Sisters there, while the other five children have more of their mother's care, more room and less danger of infection. Such cases belong to the lower border of the ungraded class. It is hard to convince the parents that no amount of school work could improve the child's mind and still harder to persuade them that institutional care is best.

Social survey of classes or groups of children. The efficacy of visiting in routine a whole group or class of children depends largely upon the amount and quality of visiting done by the teacher of the ungraded class. Some very good teachers do not seem to feel responsible for their scholars after school hours, some feel the responsibility, but lack the social spirit. Others without visible effort can build up in the families of their pupils a very real spirit of gratitude and loyalty to the ungraded class. This is what the visiting teacher must supply in the groups where the teacher has not done so; but it takes far more time than we have as yet been able to devote to this particular work.

Ideally there should be visiting teachers for all these branches of work. There should also, we think, be a social worker at the office clinics, with plenty of time to receive the parents and children, somebody who has attended other clinics and knows the horrors of the tedious but necessary waiting. Children waiting for a psychological examination should be occupied, and we feel sure the results obtained would justify the employment of a visiting teacher for this purpose.

As to the co-operation we have received, by individuals and for individuals, it has been very efficient and generous. We thank most heartily all social and settlement workers, nurses and volunteer visitors who have contributed largely to the successful results of our work, and we hope that we may be of mutual help to each other in the future.

We recommend for the future: enough workers to do for all ungraded class children what has been done for a relatively few selected cases this year.

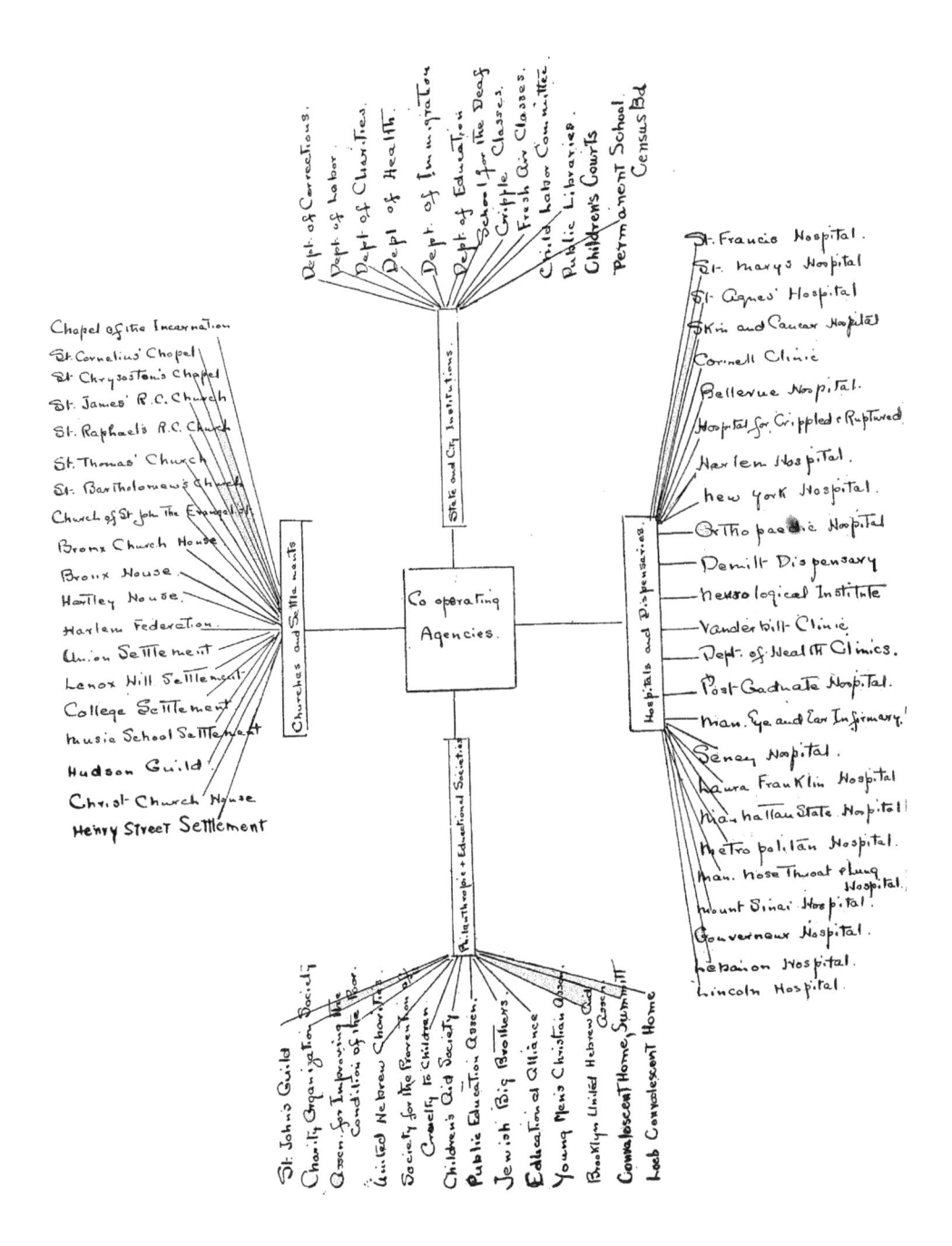

Co-operating Agencies

State and City Institutions
- Dept. of Corrections
- Dept. of Labor
- Dept. of Charities
- Dept. of Health
- Dept. of Immigration
- Dept. of Education
- School for the Deaf
- Cripple Classes
- Fresh Air Classes
- Child Labor Committee
- Public Libraries
- Children's Courts
- Permanent School Census Bd.

Churches and Settlements
- Chapel of the Incarnation
- St. Cornelius' Chapel
- St. Chrysostom's Chapel
- St. James' R.C. Church
- St. Raphael's R.C. Church
- St. Thomas' Church
- St. Bartholomew's Church
- Church of St. John the Evangelist
- Bronx Church House
- Bronx House
- Hartley House
- Harlem Federation
- Union Settlement
- Lenox Hill Settlement
- College Settlement
- Music School Settlement
- Hudson Guild
- Christ Church House
- Henry Street Settlement

Hospitals and Dispensaries
- St. Francis Hospital
- St. Mary's Hospital
- St. Agnes' Hospital
- Skin and Cancer Hospital
- Cornell Clinic
- Bellevue Hospital
- Hospital for Crippled & Ruptured
- Harlem Hospital
- New York Hospital
- Orthopaedic Hospital
- DeMilt Dispensary
- Neurological Institute
- Vanderbilt Clinic
- Dept. of Health Clinics
- Post Graduate Hospital
- Man. Eye and Ear Infirmary
- Seney Hospital
- Laura Franklin Hospital
- Manhattan State Hospital
- Metropolitan Hospital
- Man. Nose Throat & Lung Hospital
- Mount Sinai Hospital
- Gouverneur Hospital
- Lebanon Hospital
- Lincoln Hospital

Philanthropic & Educational Societies
- St. John's Guild
- Charity Organization Society
- Assn. for Improving the Condition of the Poor
- United Hebrew Charities
- Society for the Prevention of Cruelty to Children
- Children's Aid Society
- Public Education Assn.
- Jewish Big Brothers
- Educational Alliance
- Young Men's Christian Assn.
- Brooklyn United Hebrew Charities
- Convalescent Home, Summit
- Loeb Convalescent Home

COMBINED STATISTICAL REPORT OF TWO VISITING TEACHERS—UNGRADED CLASSES

No. of Classes from Which Children were Visited	Ungraded	Not Ungraded	Total
Manhattan	75	28	103
Bronx	12	1	13
Brooklyn	30	16	46
Queens	9	1	10
Richmond	...	...	...
Total	126	46	172

Sum Total	172
No. of school children visited	529
No. of children not in school visited	70
Total children visited	599
No. of home visits	1,058
Visits of co-operation (to schools, churches, settlements, etc.)	697
Total visits	1,755
Children taken to clinics and hospitals	42
No. of visits to clinics and hospitals	78

27

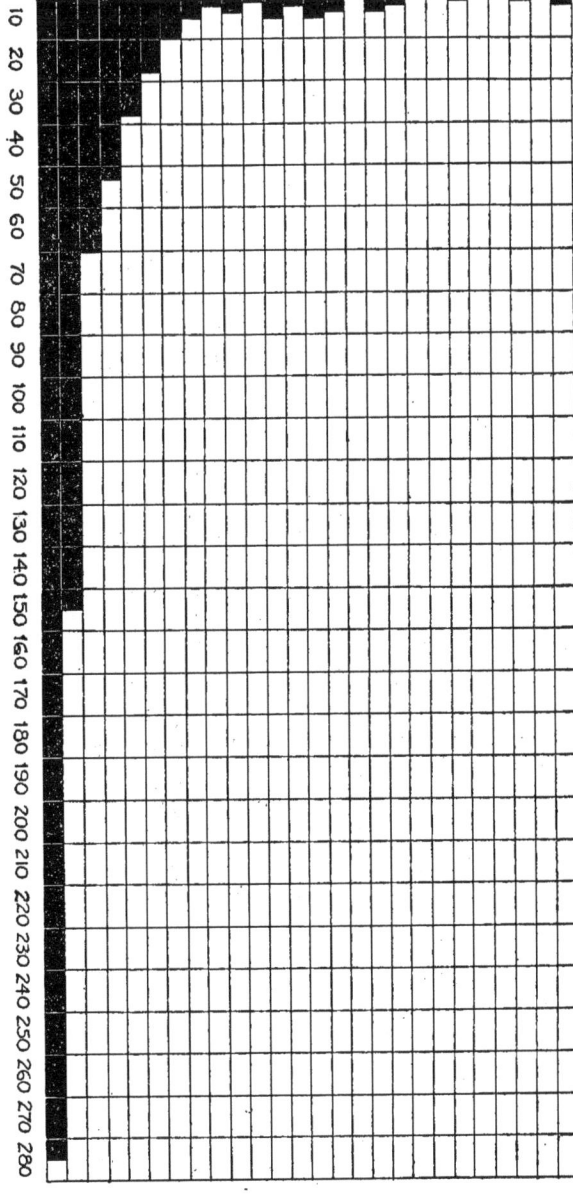

TABLE SHOWING VISITS AND REVISITS

SURVEY OF THE RESULTS OF UNGRADED CLASS WORK

It is the last mentioned field of activity, the social survey, which the visiting teacher may well develop. Her function as a Social Surveyor of the careers of those children who have left the ungraded classes at sixteen years, to enter industry, will be of the utmost importance in determining a rational program for the care of backward and defective individuals. As far as I know, there is nowhere a body of facts of this type upon which action may be based. There are persons who inform us on every occasion that the class of undesirable citizens is largely recruited from the group of backward and defective. Such talk is very largely guess work. The most definite piece of work of this kind which deals with present day verifiable facts was directed by Miss Walsh, my associate. Because of its obvious value and its pregnant meaning for the future, I bring it to your attention.

CAREERS OF 124 BOYS AND GIRLS DISCHARGED FROM UNGRADED CLASSES

In an effort to find out what becomes of those children who at sixteen years of age leave the ungraded classes, a study of eighty-six boys and thirty-eight girls has been made. Children are placed in ungraded classes after examination and certification by a physician and psychologist as being unable because of mental defect to profit by the work in the regular graded school. When children are discharged from an ungraded class a prognosis is made by the examiners. The children considered here have been out of school from one to six years; the average length of time being two years. The classes they attended were among those organized in 1906 when the department of ungraded classes was formed. The reason for choosing these older classes is obvious. More children have been discharged from them, and they have been for a longer time out in the world. The children here considered represent the total number discharged on becoming sixteen years of age from these ungraded classes.

P. S.—Lower East Side, Manhattan	8 children
P. S.—Upper " " "	9 "
P. S.—Lower " " "	8 "
P. S.—Upper " " "	9 "
P. S.—Lower " " "	12 "
P. S.— " West " "	20 "
P. S.— " East " "	7 "
P. S.— " " " "	7 "
P. S.— " " " "	9 "
P. S.—Bronx	10 "
P. S.—Ridgewood Section, Brooklyn	12 "
P. S.—Brooklyn	13 "
Total............................	124

The teachers of these classes were asked to submit a list of the names of children who had been discharged on reaching sixteen years of age. They were asked also to furnish any authentic information, not "reliable hearsay," covering the following points: kind of employment, number of jobs held, wages, number of arrests, commitment to penal institutions, number of marriages, number of children, and number of deaths. This information was checked up and augmented during the last two months by the visiting teachers from this department. In most of the cases volunteer social workers had done follow-up work in years past. There were, then, two reports on all the cases considered, and on many three.

The facts brought out by the study of these 124 cases are as follows:

Working	54%
Cared for at home (some helping)	25%
In institutions	8.8%
No information	8.9%
Dead	2.3%
Arrested	5%

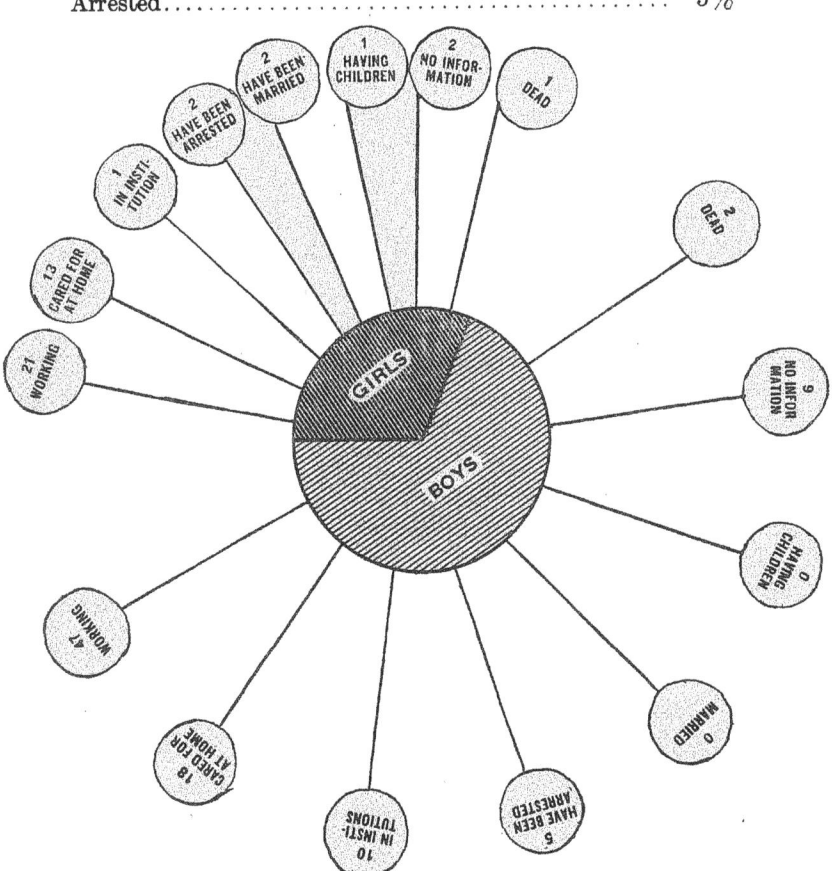

The occupations include for the girls, millinery, making of linings, factory work, laundry work, etc.; for the boys, truck driving, delivering groceries, wood turning, tailoring, etc.

The findings in this study, as far as the proportion of those who are working is concerned, agree with those referred to in a paper by Wm. A. Polglase, M. D., Medical Superintendent of the Home for Feeble-minded in Lapeer, Michigan. He says, "It has been shown that more than 50% of the adults of the higher grades of the mentally defective who have been under training from childhood are capable of doing, under intelligent supervision, a sufficient amount of work to pay for the actual cost of their support, whether in an institution or at home."

K. Richter (Leipzig), says: "Would that our master mechanics could be brought to understand that pupils sent out from our auxiliary schools (schools for mental defectives) are not nearly as incompetent as people are wont to believe; in truth they are often more capable in practical affairs than boys from the country and elsewhere. The work of training auxiliary school apprentices pays if the master does not leave the matter entirely in hands of his assistants, but looks after the boys personally and bestows the necessary patience, kindness, and oversight upon them." He has suggested a plan of following the pupils who have left the auxiliary schools. Every six years a set of questions is sent out to such of these former pupils as can be found. They seek information, especially concerning the person's ability to earn a living.

Huxley says that life is not alone a "survival of the fittest," but a "fitting of as many as possible to survive." How best may these handicapped children be helped to survive after they have been sent from the ungraded classes out into the world to earn a living? Many who have gone out have demonstrated that they are worth while. How much more they might have accomplished and how much easier their way might have been if a system of "watch-care" could have been theirs after leaving the classes. There would be a most specific value in some scheme of after supervision. For this more visiting teachers are urgently needed. Two might well spend all their time in helping to conserve these products of the ungraded classes. Some one has said the mental defectives are those who, like slag, have fallen out of nature's mould as waste material. The scientific treatment of waste material is its utilization for the best interests of the community.

We should have during the year 1915 eight additional visiting teachers in order to make this statistical and social survey on a scale which is warranted by the results of this first year of social service in the public schools.

SUMMARY OF RECOMMENDATIONS

The recommendations herein set forth may be summarized as follows:

1. The immediate demands of the Department of Ungraded Classes are:

(a) The appointment of at least four physicians, experts in nervous and mental diseases. This would in all probability make certain the examination of all children proposed by elementary school principals; the re-examination of all children in ungraded classes; and an intensive study and survey of one school district.

(b) The appointment of four assistant inspectors of ungraded classes.

(c) The appointment of eight additional visiting teachers in order that all children may have what only a few selected cases during this year have been given; that a social survey may be made of all children who have left ungraded classes.

(d) Adequate provision for clerical help. Suitable office space sufficient to meet the urgent demands of the educational clinics.

REPORT ON OPEN AIR CLASSES

Mr. William H. Maxwell,
  City Superintendent of Schools,

Dear Sir:

I present the following report on open air classes for the year 1913–14:

The open air classes this year have been of three types, classes for children with tuberculosis; the so-called "anemic" classes, which care for children who are subnormal physically or who are likely to contract tuberculosis through exposure; and the open window classes for normal children.

Each of these groups differs distinctly in its organization, its aims and in the lines along which it is conducted.

CLASSES FOR TUBERCULOUS CHILDREN

Under this heading are included those classes for children with pulmonary tuberculosis only, as the open air classes for children with bone and joint tuberculosis belong more properly to the classes for crippled children. I feel very strongly that while it is no sense necessary, or even desirable, that classes for crippled children should be put under the supervision of the physician in charge of the open air classes, it is most desirable that these children should receive their instruction in open window classes. A large proportion of these children are crippled as a result of previous bone and joint tuberculosis—in some classes as many as 40%—and all of them because of their physical handicap, get a minimum amount of out-of-doors.

NUMBER OF CASES

The classes for tuberculous children during the past school year cared for 860* cases. These children are ones who are being

*This does not represent the actual number of children, as owing to transfers and readmissions there is some duplication. Probably the actual number of children is about 15% lower than this.

treated for pulmonary tuberculosis either at Otisville, the Municipal Sanitorium for tuberculosis, or the House of Rest, or at one of the day camps for tuberculosis in the city. They are situated in the following locations:

Otisville Sanitorium...................	Annex of P. S. 14	Manhattan
House of Rest, Inwood.................	" " " 52	"
Ferry Boat, Southfield.................	" " " 14	"
" " Westfield...................	" " " 12	"
" " Middletown.................	" " " 51	"
" " Rutherford..................	" " "	Brooklyn
Vanderbilt Clinic Roof.................	" " " 141	Manhattan
East River Homes.....................	" " " 158	"

These classes are conducted entirely out of doors. The children on the day camps are in the open air eight hours daily, and at Otisville and the House of Rest open air treatment is practically continuous 24 hours a day. In all cases the children are under the direct medical supervision and charge of the nurses and physicians connected with the camp or sanitorium. They are on a high calory diet in practically all cases, and a special equipment is provided, consisting of a cot or bed for the rest hour, and clothing, consisting of sleeping bags, sweaters, overshoes, mittens, coats and caps. The exact type of equipment varies somewhat with each day camp or sanitorium, and is provided either by the institution where the day camp is operated, or, as is the case in most instances, by a private "auxiliary" or committee.

ADVANTAGES OF SCHOOLING FOR TUBERCULOUS CHILDREN

The Board of Education provides only the classroom furnishings and teachers, and receives the children for as many hours daily as in the opinion of the attending physician their physical condition permits. These classes, however, are extremely important elements in the care of these tuberculous children.

When day camps were first started, it was extremely difficult to get the parents to send the children to the camp during the school year. As few of the children had tubercle bacilli in their sputum, only a limited number could be excluded from school and the treatment would have had to be given up just as the children were beginning to make satisfactory progress. The children themselves were restless and felt keenly the loss of their education and the lack of definite mental work. Moreover the attendance was irregular as there was nothing to hold the children regularly beyond the realization (one can imagine the extent of that in childhood) that it was for their own welfare. Now the children come regularly. Attendance has improved; they are happy and contented and the parents satisfied.

Moreover the classes are of distinct economic value. A child, on account of its illness, will lose very little of its education. While in general the rate of progress is not so fast as in the regular classes, yet, as the percentage of promotions in the table at the end of the section shows, enough progress is made to prevent most of the children from losing much ground; and to enable them to qualify as wage earners within but a short time of that at which they would normally, had they kept their health and continued in the regular classes. The importance of this is realized on recalling that in the families of these children, frequently one wage earner is already incapacitated because of this disease.

As most of discharged patients fall into the groups of either apparently cured, arrested, or apparently arrested cases, the results are of very distinct value. The experience of most physicians who have had charge of day camps is that only a small percentage of cases in childhood relapse, during the school age at any rate (our experience has not yet extended over a period sufficiently long to enable us to know how permanently the resistance of these children has been raised). This means that for a period of some years (let us hope that in most cases it is for life), these children are "cured" of a disease, which, in most of them, if left to itself, would probably have gone on to a slowly progressive and fatal termination.

EFFECT OF COLD AIR

The classrooms of these children are kept at out-door temperature and the cold is not tempered by any heating. A glance at the temperature for the winter months in the classrooms on some of the day camps and at the Otisville Sanitorium shows that the children received not only fresh air, but almost frozen air for some months for their treatment.

Day Camp Temperatures

	December		January		February		March	
	Av.	Min.	Av.	Min.	Av.	Min.	Av.	Min.
Otisville.........	31.6	16	23.4	1	17.3	1	30.4	17
Rutherford.......	28	20	33	4	25	16	25	19
Westfield........	35	21	31	3	24	0	34	18
Southfield.......	44	33	32	15	40	21	49	30

Interestingly enough these months are those of their greatest improvement. While this would not justify a statement that fresh air is a valuable therapeutic agent in direct proportion to the lowness of its temperature, yet it is a fact that in tuberculosis cool and cold weather raises both the blood pressure, which is abnormally lowered by the tuberculous poison, and also the resistance of the individual; while hot weather, especially when associated with considerable humidity, lowers the general condition of the patient. The knowledge of this fact has been made use of during the past two summers, and a number of these tuberculous children have been taken to summer camps in the mountains.

One of the most successful of these summer camps has been organized, and is being conducted, through the assistance of interested private individuals, by one of the teachers of the classes for tuberculous children, and here she takes care during the summer vacation of the youngsters she teaches in the winter time. The improvement in the children in the summer is very gratifying, and from being a time of the year when they barely held their own or slipped backward a little, it is now a period of great gain.

STATISTICAL TABLES   TUBERCULOUS CLASSES

Sanitorium or Day Camp	Otisville	House of Rest	Rutherford	Southfield	Westfield	Vanderbilt Roof	East River Homes
Register 6-30-13	89	..	82	37	46	49	25
Discharged	83	..	74	42	57	80	26
Admitted	80	..	66	40	47	70	41
Register 6-30-14	86	14	72 (?)	35	36	39	40
Length of stay:							
Came once	0		1	15	0	10	0
2—29 days	3		4	8	8	20	1
30 days and over	80	Organized May 5, 1914	69	19	50	50	39
Reasons for discharge:							
To work	0		4	0	0	2	0
To school	82		46	24	21	13	24
To sanitorium or hospital	1		7	14	25	17	1
To other day camps	0		2	0	0	1	0
Too sick to attend	0		2	0	1	5	1
Not tuberculous	0		0	1	0	8	0
Other causes	0		13	3	10	34	0
Any garden (?)	Yes	..	No	Yes	Yes	Yes	Yes
Sewing, weaving, caning, etc.	Yes	..	Yes	Yes	Yes	Yes	Yes
No. hrs. daily in school	4	..	3½	3	4	3-4	5
Any exceptions	No	..	Yes	Yes	No	No	No
No. hrs. daily in camp	24	..	8	8	9	8	..
Length of rest hour	Varies	..	1½	1½	1	2	¾
Per cent. attendance							
school days	98	..	83.8	..	81	85	88
Seven days a week	100	..	76	..	78	80	..
Summer vacation	..	..	81	..	61	85	60
Per cent. promotions:							
6-30-13	..	..	85	73	65	80	92
1-31-14	90	..	83	56	70	67	89
6-30-14	68	..	82	80	70	62	84

ANEMIC CLASSES

In the classes for tuberculous children we saw a type of class which was associated with an enterprise whose aims were curative. The anemic class stands for both prevention and cure—prevention of the disease which the classes for tuberculous children were organized to aid in combating, and as an aid in restoring to health those children whose physical condition seems distinctly below the normal standard.

At the close of this year there are 39 anemic classes connected with the following schools:

SCHOOLS HAVING ANEMIC CLASSES

Manhattan 12, 17, 21, 33 (2 classes), 51 (2 classes), 61, 65B, 84, 89, 92, 95, 107, 110, 179, 192.

Brooklyn 5, 8, 30, 34, 85, 91, 150, 162 (3 classes), 168, 173 (2 classes), 174, 175.

Bronx 4, 45, 46.

Queens 7, 90, 92.

Richmond 13.

These classes are situated, with one or two exceptions, on school property and the classes are under the medical supervision of a physician officially connected with the educational system. The classes are limited to 25 children, and in a number of cases the register is held somewhat lower. This is deemed necessary, on account of the educational difficulties connected with teaching so many grades.

Most of these classes are indoors, in classrooms of more than average size, which have the windows pivoted. Some have roofs or balconies in connection with them which may be used in favorable weather. Three or four have only out-door classrooms, and have to find some makeshift quarters when the weather is too severe or stormy to permit being out-of-doors. This is occasionally necessary, as the present equipment does not protect adequately against severe cold. Moreover when children come to school in wet clothing, as they sometimes do in a cold winter rain, it is not possible to have them sit out in the raw atmosphere in their wet clothes.

TEMPERATURE OF CLASS ROOMS

Some heat is permitted in the class rooms when necessary to overcome unduly low temperature or excessive dampness. There is a distinctly rational use for it in the latter condition, as cold moist air radiates body heat much quicker than cold dry air. Thus a temperature of 32 degrees F. with much moisture will chill a child much more quickly than one of 20 to 25 degrees with little moisture. The temperature rarely goes below 35 to 30 degrees F. in these class rooms.

KIND AND SITUATION OF OPEN AIR CLASS ROOMS

A general tendency throughout the country seems to be to place anemic children entirely out of doors. With the changeable climate of New York City, and the extremely raw weather in winter, I am distinctly in favor of keeping the classes within buildings. Apart from that, to get an out-door or roof structure of sufficient rigidity to insure any permanency or stability requires a very considerable expenditure. Even then it is difficult so to construct such shelters as to render them satisfactory in both cold and warm weather, and in New York City we have, during the school year, extremes in temperature. In the cold weather it is desirable to have a shelter so arranged as to permit the sides being adjusted to keep out all wind, with the top so constructed that it may roll back completely, thus allowing a maximum of sunshine on the children and a minimum of air movement. Such a condition approaches the ideal for cold weather.

On the other hand, in warm weather the sides need to be raised as much as possible to permit a maximum air movement, and even under such conditions, if a double roof with an intervening air space is not present, the temperature is apt to become very high under the shelter.

It is difficult to construct a type of shelter which will satisfactorily meet both of these requirements. One made of canvas may be constructed which will give moderate satisfaction in summer. In winter, however, too much air can get through the joints on windy days, and besides there is danger, if the weather turns cold after a heavy rain, of the canvas freezing and being ripped into shreds if a high wind follows. This has been the fate of one or two such structures already in use, in the storms of last winter. One other objection to roof structure, and in my mind a serious one, is the physical strain to which the children are subjected when the class is put on the roof of the school building. To reach the roof of one of the newer school buildings necessitates a climb of five or six flights of stairs. This climb has to be made twice daily by the children in the anemic classes so situated. The anemic classes contain children from the lower grades as well as the upper, and they are children in poor physical condition. I think the expenditure of effort needed to climb these stairs is distinctly undesirable.

In addition, the placing of any children with cardiac disease in classes so situated is absolutely contraindicated. Personally, I am more in favor of a class situated on about the third floor in a corner room with preferably an easterly and southerly exposure. This gives a maximum of sunlight in winter and the heat and glare of the sun in hot weather can be tempered by shades. Of course, it is desirable in placing a class on the third floor to be assured that the buildings opposite are not so high as to cut off the sunlight during some of the winter months when the sun's angle with the horizon is rather small.

PROPER EQUIPMENT OF ROOMS AND CLOTHING OF CHILDREN

Besides, as stated before, the present equipment does not protect adequately against very low temperature, and one that would do so is too expensive. To protect children properly against extreme cold or wind, two features are necessary in the equipment which are lacking in that of the anemic classes in the public schools. The first of these is a coat or sweater of some warm material which is a good non-conductor. One of the best materials for these garments is angora wool. It combines the minimum of weight with the maximum of warmth. As it is loosely woven it is desirable to provide over it a garment of closely woven kahki-like material which is so made as to be practically wind-proof. Garments such as these are in use in some of the open-air classes in the private schools in New York City, and have proved satisfactory. The cost of these is about $8.00 greater than that of the present equipment, and as the angora sweaters are all wool they require an expensive method of cleaning to prevent matting and shrinkage. The equipment as supplied by the Board of Education, together with the approximate cost of each article, is as follows:

Moulthrop chairs, at	$5.50	each
Folding cots at	2.00	"
Sleeping bags, at	4.50	"
Sweaters, at	1.25	"
Caps, at	.25	"
Overshoes, at	2.25	a pair
Mittens, at	.20	"
	$15.95	

RESULTS ON PHYSICAL CONDITION

The effect of these classes on the physical condition of the children has already been set forth in the detailed reports of the careful studies made during the past three years, and has been incorporated in your annual reports of 1911-12-13.

A few points, however, are worthy of mention outside of the data contained in the appended table. One of these is the slight influence of feeding this year on the gain in weight.

In Manhattan, in six classes where feeding was given, the average gain was 2.7 lbs., while the average gain in eight where no feeding was given was 3.3 lbs. The schools in all the other boroughs gave feeding, with the exception of P. S. No. 4, in the Bronx, but the average of these schools which did not include a substantial lunch, but merely milk, cocoa, crackers, etc., was 2.9 lbs. In the other five schools, four in Brooklyn and one in Richmond, where a substantial lunch was given in addition, the average gain was 5.8 lbs. The following menu, however, which was used at P. S. No.

150, Brooklyn, is much greater than could be introduced into fresh air classes in general.

10 A. M., cereal with milk and sugar or cocoa with crackers.

12 Noon, thick soup with meat, fish or eggs. Cocoa, bread. Sometimes fruit.

2:15 P. M., milk with crackers.

The daily cost is about $12\frac{1}{2}$ cents per capita, of which the children pay only about $\frac{1}{3}$. In Richmond the Parents Association of P. S. No. 13 contributed $400 last year for food and clothing for these children. In Manhattan the feeding was practically self supporting. In general, the results this year seem to bear out the impression our previous studies gave us that the addition of milk and crackers or some light form of nourishment in the morning or afternoon, or both, seems to have but little effect upon the general progress of these children, and not very much upon the weight.

The improvement in scholarship is also very encouraging. Many children made normal progress who previously had failed. Over 50 advanced more rapidly than the normal rate, though no attempt was made to goad the children to additional effort, and children are always encouraged to rest whenever they feel tired. Of course it is difficult to determine how much of the improvement in scholarship is due to gain in health and ability to concentrate and work, and how much is due to the additional individual attention these pupils may receive.

The average attendance of these classes is excellent, considering that these are children whose physical conditions renders them more likely than the majority of those in school to contract illness. In most cases the attendance approximates closely to that of the school as a whole.

PERMANENCY OF RESULTS

Of necessity it occurs at times to all of us who are working in any branch of public health service, to wonder whether what we accomplish is really worth the effort expended, and whether our results are anything more than temporary.

The endeavor to get some data on this question, led me to gather together those children whom I could, who had been discharged from the anemic class at P. S. No. 21, Manhattan, where, on account of the length of time the class had been in operation, I could get the greatest number of cases. Thirty-five of these discharged cases were still in the school. They had been out of the class from one to three years. Superficial examination showed nearly all of them to be in good physical condition. Their color was good and they carried themselves as if they had plenty of reserve energy and good physical tone.

Examination showed that they had gained on an average of 16 pounds in weight since leaving the class, and that their average hemoglobin was 90 per cent. Compare this with 72 to 77 per cent., the averages of the class on admission. Their hemoglobin had increased on an average of 7.8 per cent. Only eight out of thirty-five had lost in hemoglobin, and of these in six cases it was only from 1 to 5 per cent. Only eight showed a hemoglobin below 85 per cent. and none below 81 per cent.

In a word, the findings encouragingly lead us to the conclusion that we are engaged in a work that is of distinct benefit to the children, and one in which the results, so far as can be determined from a very limited number of cases, show a surprising degree of permanency.

NEED FOR MORE ANEMIC CLASSES

The need for additional classes for anemic children is great, especially in certain localities. This is particularly true of that great section of the East Side in Manhattan, from Delancey Street, north, to the Harlem River, and bounded on the east by the Bowery and Third Avenue. In this immense and over-crowded area there is only one anemic class. Requests have been made in the Budget for funds for additional classes in this district and it cannot be too strongly urged that they be granted.

STATISTICAL TABLES—ANEMIC CLASSES

School	No. Children Registered	No. School Days in Operation	Percentage of Attendance	Feeding	Wt. Av. Gain	Ht. Av. Gain	Scholarship No. Children Making More than Grade	Grade	Less than Grade	Comparison with Progress Prior to Entering Class
Manhattan										
12......	21	184	97	12 oz. milk, rolls or bread	3.6 lbs.	.86 in.	4	10	8	Improvement. Same in most cases.
17......	23	187½	89	Milk and rolls or bread..	3.2 "	1 "	1	18	4	Better in 4 cases.
21......	20	179	90	None................	4.04 "	1.58 "	2	12	3	Improvement. Seven who were repeaters advanced normally.
33 (2 cl.)	49	152½	86	Buttered rolls or sandwiches, some milk, cocoa or soup........	2.3 "	.85 "	5	33	12	Improvement.
51 (2 cl.)	52	188	87	None................	4.01 "	1.56 "	3	41	8	Improvement.
61......	24	148	91	None................	3.55 "	1.41 "	4	16	4	Improvement.
*65B....	24	64	92	None................	1.29 "	.57 "	..	20	4	About same.
√84.....	24	133	79	Milk and crackers......	3.21 "	.85 "	..	20	4	50% better progress. 50% same
92......	24	9½ mos.	90	None...... 12/15/13–6/30/14	4.66 lbs.	.62 in.	2	19	3	....
95......	23	201(?)	87	Crackers and milk for two months......	3.48 "	.49 "	2	20	1	Improvement.
107.....	22	184	85	Milk and crackers at 10 A. M........	3.42 "	.77 "	1	15	6	Some improvement.
179.....	20	123	88	None................	6.3 "	....	3	17	..	Improvement.

*Started 2/2/14. √ Organized 10/24/13.

STATISTICAL TABLES—ANEMIC CLASSES—*Continued*

School	No. Children Registered	No. School Days in Operation	Percentage of Attendance	Feeding	Wt. Av. Gain	Ht. Av. Gain	Scholarship No. Children Making More than Grade	Grade	Less than Grade	Comparison with Progress Prior to Entering Class
Brooklyn 5......	25	120	84	Milk, sandwiches, cheese, buns, jelly, gingerbread, fruit, muffins..	5.4 lbs.	2.2 in.				
8......	23	92	84	One pint milk, 4 crackers	3.6 "	1.5 "	2	22	1	Improvement.
34......	23	165	86	Boiled rice, soup, custard stewed fruits............	4.8 "	2 "	2	16	5	?
85......	20	196	100(?)	Milk and crackers........	2 "	? "	3	12	8	Improvement.
91......	25	91	80	Milk, Sept. to Jan.; Jan. to April, soup, bread and cocoa; April and May, milk and crackers			1	11	9	?
150......	17	244	86	ers; June, milk..... Milk, cereal, 10 A. M.; substantial lunch; milk	8 "	2.3 "	3	26	5	Improvement.
162...... (3 classes)	66	151	78	and crackers, 2:15 P.M. Milk, cocoa, soup, oatmeal............	7.6 "	3.9 "	..	16	1	Improvement.
173...... (2 classes)	50	193	84	Soup, cocoa, milk, crackers............	3.5 "	......	..	..	..	....
174......	25	107	89	Milk or cocoa and crackers............	4 "	.2 in.	..	22	3	Improvement.
					1.8 " 5/1–6/15	.08 " 1/1–6/15	2	14	9	Some improvement

STATISTICAL TABLES—ANEMIC CLASSES—*Continued*

School	No. Children Registered	No. School Days in Operation	Percentage of Attendance	Feeding	Wt. Av. Gain	Ht. Av. Gain	Scholarship No. Children Making More than Grade	Grade	Less than Grade	Comparison with Progress Prior to Entering Class
Started Dec., 1913										
Bronx 4......	27	189	94	None............	2.5 lbs.	1 in.	0	21	3	Improvement.
45......	26	188(?)	87	Pint of milk and 2 crackers..........	No scales	No scales	1	17	8	Some improvement.
46......	22	?	86	Cocoa and crackers.....	2.3 lbs.	.08 in.	1	20	1	About same.
Queens 7......	18	68	70	Milk and crackers......	1 "	.5 "	0	16	2	Improved.
92......	20	100	86	Milk............	2.1 "	No record	1	17	3	About same.
Richmond 13......	24	118	86	Milk and crackers, 9 and 3; lunch at 12........	4.1 "	No record	0	23	13	Improvement.

45

OPEN WINDOW CLASSES FOR NORMAL CHILDREN

It had seemed to me on visiting schools in the springtime that the children in the regular classes were in poorer physical condition than in the fall. Many teachers complained of being exhausted at the close of the school day and in poor health at the end of the year. A considerable number of these teachers ascribed their condition to the artificial methods of ventilation employed.

Studies of air conditions in the class rooms revealed the fact that in most of them as measured by present ventilating standards they were very good. Yet the fact remained that teachers and children seemed to become "run down" during the winter, while children already subnormal physically improved in the fresh air classes for anemic children, and that the teachers of these classes reported themselves in much better condition at the end of the school year than prior to taking the classes.

On this account, and because of the success of the open-window class for normal children at P. S. No. 9, Manhattan, and because of the interest of teachers in the movement and the impossibility of providing anemic classes for the many applicants for them, the organization of open-window classes in considerable numbers was undertaken.

Suggestions, made about the end of the first term, to start such classes were received with approval by some principals and district superintendents, and the movement was taken up with enthusiasm. Classes of this type were given to teachers who desired to teach in the open air. During February and March classes were rapidly organized, so that for a good part of last term there were ninety such classes situated in the following schools in Manhattan:

No.	3	2 Classes	(E)	
"	6	1 "	"	
"	9	1 "	Regular Grade	
"	12	9 "	"	"
"	14	1	E	
"	18	2	Regular	
"	19	7	"	
"	50	2	"	

No.	53	1 Classes	Regular	
"	54	1 "	"	
"	59	8 "	"	(incl. kind.)
	70	3		
	73	12	"	and 1 C class. 1 Ungraded
	76	3		
	77	2		
	84	14	"	and 2 E classes
	88	1		
"	96P	4 "	"	
"	96G	2		
"	104	1 "		
"	116	2		
"	122	2 "		
"	135	3	"	
"	158	1	E	
"	179	1 "	Regular	
"	183	4 "	"	
"	45 (Bronx)	1 "	"	

These classes were conducted like ordinary classes, except that the classrooms were cut out of the ventilating system, and ventilation was carried out by means of open windows. This gave, during the winter, a lower temperature, greater humidity, and greater air movement, as well as that intangible quantity, "fresh air." The classroom temperature was kept between 50 and 60 degrees F. when the outside temperature was not higher, and 50 degrees F. was considered the minimum temperature. Heat was permitted to overcome unduly low temperatures and "rawness" (excessive humidity). Children were allowed to wear their own wraps and hats when they desired, but no equipment was provided. In some classes feeding was given at the desire of teachers or principals. This was almost entirely self-supporting. It consisted either of food, such as sandwiches, brought by the children, with or without milk, or else milk and crackers, procured by the teacher and for which the children paid. The average cost when milk was procured by the teacher was about ten cents per capita per week.

In all cases the consents of the parents to put their children into classes so conducted were obtained. In some classes the children were weighed. As this was not general, and was done in most cases on outside scales with the first weight in winter clothing and the last in summer clothing, no attempt has been made to analyze these data. In fact, the classes have been organized too short a time to permit of any definite conclusions being drawn.

IMPRESSIONS OF TEACHERS OF OPEN-WINDOW CLASSES

The impressions of the teachers, however, are interesting, and there is sufficient unanimity of opinion in a large number of cases to be suggestive. Of course, as in any movement which is taken up in a burst of enthusiasm, there was bound to be some reaction. However, only twelve of the ninety teachers had any decided objections to the classes, and it is worthy of note that five of these were from one school. All these five objected on the ground that they thought the children too poorly clad, and required feeding which was not given. Two others objected on account of throat or ear trouble. Three on account of cold. This was due to unsuitable rooms, either northern exposure or drafts. One objected to the noise. As this same noise must be present in all the classrooms in that wing of the building during at least two months of the school year when the windows are open, it would suggest that some decided action might be desirable to reduce the amount of noise, if possible, in the neighborhood of that particular school building.

A good deal of complaint came at first on damp days particularly before some of the teachers realized that they could turn on the heat if they desired. Advice as to reducing air circulation and raising temperature on such days reduced such complaints to a minimum.

Outside of this the children seemed to notice the cold very little. Even when their hands felt cold to the touch they asserted that they were comfortable, and there were only occasional complaints on a damp day if there was a draft across the floor on their feet.

A few reports from some of the teachers who found the classes satisfactory may be of interest. In the first place there were fifty-eight teachers who expressed themselves as of the opinion that the classes had had a beneficial effect on either themselves or the children. In nearly all these cases they agreed that the children were less listless, more energetic, and before long looked better. Some teachers thought that some particularly sickly-looking children improved very markedly. The following reports are of especial interest:

The teacher of one class which was started the first of January reports: "Children very much brighter, more active, more responsive. Self, very much stronger, appetite improved. Never feel so tired and exhausted at the end of the day as I did formerly. Would not wish to give up open window class under any circumstances while possible to keep it."

Another states, "For the past few years I have been troubled with tonsilitis. This year, not at all. The effect upon some of the children has been very marked. A few of my children were out a great deal last term on account of coughs and colds. Very rarely have the children had colds this term, with the same class."

Another, "I have gained about 20 pounds, due in part to the fresh air. I am not nearly so fatigued at the end of the day. I have been free from colds."

Still another, "have kept normal weight, whereas other years have found me considerably less at end of term."

A teacher of one of the ungraded classes reports for herself a "gain of one inch in chest measurement, could eat four meals a day, and sleep better. I gained six pounds very soon. Felt less nervous, had better control of class. They were less restless, less apathetic, cried out for 'air' if I forgot it for a moment."

A 2B teacher says: "The parents were enthusiastic about their children's improved health. It showed in rosier cheeks and increased appetites. Good effect on class and teacher."

Another second year teacher states: "The open air had a very beneficial effect on the children, both physically and mentally. As for myself, I have never been in better condition at the end of June."

The teacher of a special E class reports: "I belive this sort of a class has been very beneficial to the children of this special class. They seem to study with more energy than other special classes I have had."

SUGGESTIONS FOR MANAGEMENT OF OPEN-WINDOW CLASSES

For the benefit of those who may be planning to take up this type of work, perhaps some of the following suggestions, based on our experience during the past year, may prove of some help.

1. That room is preferable for this type of a class which has windows on two sides so as to insure open windows on at least one side, if on account of high winds or a driving storm they have to be closed on the other. Rooms with sliding doors such as those which form parts of assembly rooms are not satisfactory. The doors do not fit closely together and this, together with the ventilator above, creates too much of a draft.

2. A room with south or east exposure gives best results, as this room is the warmest in winter time. Rooms with a northern exposure, particularly those rooms in which it is difficult to keep the temperature at a comfortable point in cold weather with the windows closed are bound to give dissatisfaction.

3. A minimum of 50 degrees F. seems to yield the best results, as under ordinary conditions children do not feel cold at this temperature. On some cold raw days without sun, the temperature will need to be higher, probably over 55 degrees. It is well to assume that shivering on the part of any child indicates that the child is not warm enough.

4. In order that the children with their extra wraps may not be overheated, the temperature should not be allowed to go above 58 to 60 degrees, unless the outside temperature is so high as to render this impossible. As an aid to teachers in watching temperatures, it is suggested that the red marking on the new thermometers in the school rooms might be adjusted in classrooms of this type so as to point to 50 and 58 degrees, instead of 60 and 68 degrees, as in the ordinary classrooms.

5. The children and teachers will feel more comfortable if the doors and the transoms are kept closed. It is necessary that the tramsoms should fit tight and not be warped, as otherwise distinct drafts are apt to ensue. There are three conditions under which exceptions might be desirable.

a. If in raw severe weather it should be impossible to keep the temperature of the room about 50, even with plenty of heat, then if the children complain of cold the windows might have to be closed. Under these circumstances the doors and transoms should be kept open to insure sufficient ventilation.

b. If the children come to school with their clothing soaking wet, it is desirable that the room be conducted as a closed classroom until their clothing is dry, unless the temperature with the windows open is about 65 degrees or higher.

c. As we believe in these classes some of the benefits are obtained by preventing overheating, it is desirable in warmer weather, if, even with the heat off, the temperature goes above 70 degrees, that the transoms or doors, or both, should be kept open to insure better air circulation, and consequently better radiation of body heat.

6. It is desirable to have it understood that it is necessary to have some of the windows in the room open both top and bottom to insure proper ventilation, as there is a tendency on raw days for some teachers to keep all the bottom sashes closed. In some cases, if opening lower sashes makes too great a breeze on the heads of the children near them, this can be avoided by tacking heavy unbleached muslin along the lower part of the window frame, or if a manual training class exists in the school, by having a board made to fit across the opening in a manner somewhat similar to that of some of the commercial ventilators now on the market.

7. The heat required to maintain the temperature at approximately 50 to 55 degrees, should be obtained preferably by a little heat from each radiator, rather than by all from one radiator, so as to prevent any child sitting near a radiator from being overheated. This is practicable, as in most classrooms the radiators have valves which can be controlled by the teachers. All children should be urged to wear sweaters if they can obtain them. They should be allowed to put on wraps or overcoats if they feel the need of them. Children with catarrh or running ears or whose medical card shows adenoids should be placed on that side of the room

away from the open window. Those susceptible to catarrh or those near windows should be encouraged to wear caps, regardless of appearance.

8. At that time of the year, particularly in the spring, when it is said that " all rooms are open-window rooms," children should not be allowed to dress more warmly than in an ordinary classroom. Unless prevented by the teacher, many children will keep on coats or sweaters on days when the temperature is well over 70 degrees in the classroom. To children so dressed there is serious danger of overheating, with the attending depressing physical effects which the classes are endeavoring to counteract.

9. It is advisable that teachers dress appropriately. A thin wash waist, which is comfortable in a hot steam-heated apartment, is not sufficient for such a room, and unless teachers wear flannel waists or sweaters they will want to keep the temperature too warm for the more warmly clad children. There is a tendency, I think, for most of us to forget that, except in cases of extreme poverty, the average public school children who come from homes where there is no heating plant are accumstomed to dress very much more warmly than those of us who live in steam-heated apartments, where the temperature nearly always tends to be too high.

10. Physical exercise should be more frequent than in the regular room, emphasizing deep breathing, respiratory and circulatory movements.

11. It is not desirable, if pupils show unusual mental alertness as a result of the open air, that they should be overtaxed. Any tendency to turn classes of this kind into rapid advancement classes should be discouraged.

Our short experience with this type of class indicates that they are going to prove distinctly helpful in bettering the physical condition of both children and teachers. I think they may be made of especial value in those over-crowded schools in which the "anemic classes" are needed, but in which there is no available room. These schools have frequently several classes of the same grade. I believe that half a loaf is better than none, and that while we cannot obtain the rest and the special routine of an anemic class, yet if we can have one open-window room to the grade, where several classes to the grade exist and can place in this room a classful of those children whose physical condition seems poorest, we are going to improve their general health to a considerable degree.

PROBLEMS OF VENTILATION

Probably one of the most important effects of the fresh air classes is the aid they have been in producing distinctly new view points in considering the problems of ventilation.

Whereas heretofore the standards of adequate and healthful ventilation have been based on physical and chemical conditions of the atmosphere, there is a tendency to substitute at least in part for them a physiological standard, based on the effects of the surroundings on the individual. Whereas heretofore air conditions had to be healthful because they conformed to certain arbitrary standards, in the future, air conditions will probably be considered good, because in them, as the result of observation, it has been concluded that individuals keep most healthy.

That open window methods of ventilation will be the only ones under which healthful conditions can be obtained; that modern scientific investigation will not discover in-door conditions which shall be such as to keep the individual's condition at the optimum, I do not believe. Civilization, which demands that we spend a good part of time in doors, will also demand that we spend that time both healthfully and comfortably, and will demand that we do not have to be personally concerned in the details of ventilation necessary to make us so. However, open window methods and the results which they have accomplished have been an important factor in putting us on the road towards something better in indoor living for large groups of individuals, than anything we have heretofore known.

In conclusion, I wish to express my deepest appreciation of the courtesy and assistance received from all members of the school system with which I have come in contact, from the Committee on the Prevention of Tuberculosis, from the Bureau of Child Hygiene, Department of Health, and from the physicians in charge of the various tuberculosis day camps. Without the assistance of all of these my work and this report could have been very inadequately rendered.

Respectfully submitted,

I. OGDEN WOODRUFF,
Medical Inspector Open Air Classes.

CLASSES FOR BLIND CHILDREN

NEW YORK, July 14, 1914

MR. WILLIAM H. MAXWELL,
City Superintendent of Schools,

DEAR SIR:

I have the honor to submit herewith a report of the Classes for Blind Children for the year ending July 31, 1914:

The work for blind children suffered a severe loss through the death, on November 17, 1913, of Miss Gertrude E. Bingham, the first Inspector and organizer of this department in the public schools of New York City. By her untiring efforts and deep devotion such successful results had been obtained as to unquestionably prove the wisdom of educating blind children side by side with their sighted brothers and sisters. Following along the lines which she had so wisely marked out, the work has steadily progressed during the past year.

STATISTICS

Register of Pupils—1913–14:

Manhattan	101
Brooklyn	68
The Bronx	13
Queens	12
Total	194

Number of pupils discharged during the year:

Graduated	2
Transferred to an ungraded class	1
Transferred to regular classes	2
Moved out of the city	4
Admitted to homes for the blind	2
Over age and left school to go to work	6
Died	2
Total	19

Number of pupils admitted during the year:

Totally blind	16
With defective vision	28
Total	44

ELEMENTARY SCHOOLS

A class for blind children was opened in Public School 136, Brooklyn, in April, 1914.

The enrollment of the class for blind children in Public School 17, Manhattan, having increased to 18, an additional class was established in that school on May 4, 1914, for the remainder of the term. A substitute teacher was employed to assist the regular teacher of the blind, who had supervision of both classes. The pupils in this additional class will be transferred to Public School 44, Manhattan, where a class for blind children will be opened September 14, 1914.

The blind children in the elementary schools have made gratifying progress, in several cases standing at the head of their respective classes.

HIGH SCHOOLS

In February, 1913, three blind pupils, two boys and a girl, were graduated from elementary schools. One boy was admitted to the Boys' High School, Brooklyn, and the other to the High School of Commerce, Manhattan. The girl could not afford to attend high school at this time and secured work at the New York Association for the Blind, but expects to enter Washington Irving High School in September.

Of the six blind pupils enrolled in high schools in September, 1913, three have continued their courses, two left to take up manual work, and the other graduated and has entered Columbia University.

This latter pupil's record at the De Witt Clinton High School, Manhattan, shows how high the possibilities of attainment for

P. S. 20, MAN. BLIND CHILDREN WITH SEEING CHILDREN. KINDERGARTEN. NOV. 13, 1913, G975.

blind pupils can be raised. He graduated at the head of his class, receiving a gold medal for high special honors. In Latin, German, English and History his marks were 90 per cent. or over during the entire course. He is totally blind, commuted every day from his home in Bayside, L. I., and completed the regular four years' course in three years.

Monthly conferences with the special teachers have been held throughout the year.

WORK IN THE PRINTING OFFICE FOR THE BLIND

The output from the printing office during the year is as follows:

Embossed brass plates for new Braille books..... 2,646
Printed pages.................................. 32,307

(This equals, approximately, 645 bound volumes—50 pages to a volume.)

VOCATIONAL TRAINING

To educate, in the ordinary meaning of the work, a normal blind child is a comparatively easy matter, but to educate in the broader sense, that is, to fit him for a useful and successful life, is a very difficult task. So few occupations are possible for a person lacking sight and competition is so keen in those open to him that the most thorough education is hardly sufficient to start a blind boy or girl on the road to success.

Much is being said and done in the line of vocational education at the present time. Please allow me to call your attention to this great need for our blind children.

A blind student blessed with a brilliant mentality and comfortable home conditions may, after graduating from high school and college, earn his living by working in a profession or along literary lines. For these few gifted children the public schools in our city offer unexcelled advantages. The mentally slow blind child receives sufficient instruction in handwork to give him a start in the only occupations, such as chair caning, basketry, broom mak-

A WRITTEN LESSON. BLIND BOY WRITING BRAILLE WITH BRAILLE SLATE AND STYLUS.

ing, rug weaving, etc., possible for him. For the great majority of blind children, who fall between these two extremes, not enough vocational training has been provided. Through long experience the institutions for the blind have found that music in its various forms offers the best opportunities for their charges. No provision is made by the Board of Education for this form of vocational education. This lack has been provided for in a measure by the New York and Brooklyn Associations for the Blind. They have given instruction to forty-seven public school children, of our classes for blind children, during the past year: Thirty-seven on the piano, six on the piano and violin, three in voice and piano and one on the cornet.

The New York Association for the Blind, in conjunction with the Music School Settlement, has also provided instruction for several former pupils in piano tuning and repairing. We wish to express our gratitude for this great help which has been given our pupils by these associations.

The work of these associations along these lines is necessarily limited by lack of time and accommodations. Therefore, I beg leave to recommend the appointment of a special teacher of music to give instruction to the older blind pupils in both instrumental music and piano tuning.

Five of our pupils this spring won scholarships offered by the National Conservatory of Music of America. Of these, one girl will receive vocal instruction, two boys piano lessons, and two boys instruction upon the violin during the coming year.

PHYSICAL TRAINING—ATHLETICS

The work in physical training has followed the same broad lines as heretofore. Much interest is shown in athletics. In the championship games held at Madison Square Garden last winter, a blind boy from Public School 171, Manhattan, was in the finals for the 100-yard dash. At the fête held in Central Park June 8th, nine blind girls from Public School 17, Manhattan, danced with sighted partners. They kept together so well that it was impossible to distinguish the sightless dancers from the others.

LECTURES FOR BLIND CHILDREN

The lectures especially prepared for our blind children by the American Museum of Natural History during the year were greatly enjoyed by those who were able to attend.

EYE EXAMINATIONS

Through the co-operation of the Sight Saving Service of the New York Association for the Blind, 121 public school children were examined during the year at special weekly clinics held by Dr. Ellice M. Alger, Professor of Diseases of the Eye at the Post-Graduate Hospital. Of this number 43 were pupils in our classes for blind children. Thirty-seven were not attending school because of eye trouble and 41 were brought for examination by a school visitor of the Public Education Association. Of the 37 not attending school, 23 were admitted to the classes for blind children, 10, after examination and treatment, were able to return to their regular classes, and four, who were over 14 years of age, secured employment. Complete records are kept on file and have proved of great value in dealing intelligently with each case.

The great service rendered us by Dr. Alger deserves a hearty note of thanks.

Glasses were prescribed for 46 children. Where parents were unable to purchase glasses for their children, they were procured through private contributions. A small sum of money placed, yearly, in the hands of the Associate Superintendent in Charge of Classes for Blind Children to provide such glasses, would yield a large return by increasing the efficiency of children suffering from curable defects of vision.

Respectfully submitted

S. FLORENCE WARREN,

Acting Inspector, Classes for the Blind.

SCHOOL FOR THE DEAF

Mr. WILLIAM H. MAXWELL,

    City Superintendent of Schools,

DEAR SIR:

I have the honor to submit my report for the year 1913–1914 on the work of the School for the Deaf.

STATISTICS

Register	Boys	Girls	Total
June 30, 1913—Manhattan	127	110	237
Brooklyn	10	8	18
Queens	5	3	8
Total	142	121	263
June 30, 1914—Manhattan	132	118	250
Brooklyn	13	6	19
Queens	8	7	15
Total	153	131	284

No. of classes June 30, 1913:
    Manhattan............... 25
    Brooklyn................ 2
    Queens.................. 1
                        28

No. of classes June 30, 1914:
    Manhattan............... 28
    Brooklyn................ 2
    Queens.................. 1
                        31

Seventy children have been admitted to the school during the school year. Each year we receive an increased number of children from regular schools who have lost ground through partial deafness. These children become alert and happy and find that they can do well when under proper conditions. The regular school gains, too, by being relieved of children who are a drag.

There have been more discharges than usual because a number of pupils over 16 years of age were compelled to go to work. Of the children discharged

    5 were graduates.
    17 went to work.
    11 went to institutions, because of poor home surroundings.
    6 moved out of the city.
    1 was too ill to attend.
    3 were transferred to regular schools.
    3 went to private schools.
    2 died.
    1 (over age) is staying at home.

The school keeps in touch with all the pupils who have left it and reports show they are working earnestly and in many cases doing very well.

The Brooklyn classes have held their own and the Queens class has almost doubled; but I think these children would gain more rapidly if they were in the central school and could have the advantage of better grading and regular industrial work.

ORIGIN AND DISTRIBUTION OF DEAFNESS

AGE AT WHICH DEAFNESS OCCURRED

    87 were born deaf.
    86 became deaf before the third year.
    65 became deaf before the sixth year.
    46 became deaf after they were six years old.

This table shows that 60 per cent. of the school must acquire speech and language.

CAUSES OF DEAFNESS

87 are congenitals.
76 are deaf from spinal meningitis.
38 are deaf from scarlet fever.
10 are deaf from convulsions.
12 are deaf from falls and blows.
4 are deaf from typhoid.
7 are deaf from brain fever.
9 are deaf as a result of measles.
5 are deaf from infantile paralysis.
4 are deaf from abscesses.
7 are deaf from catarrh.
3 are deaf from pneumonia.
10 a gradual loss of hearing.
12 unknown.

These children are not only deaf, but they are physically not strong. They shuffle their feet and have a poor gait. Their physical training must be considered very carefully.

AMOUNT OF DEAFNESS

156 are totally deaf.
120 can hear loud sounds.
8 can hear the voice at close range.

WHERE CHILDREN COME FROM

168 from Manhattan.
63 from Brooklyn.
27 from the Bronx.
20 from Queens.
5 from Richmond.
1 from out of town.

The daily traveling to and from school has given these children self reliance and has brought them in constant contact with hearing people. The older children take care of the little ones and there have been no accidents. The more normal we can make these children the better able they will be to take a place in the world and to keep it. The world shows little sympathy for the deaf. The affliction of blindness or lameness is apparent and arouses instant desire to help, but people grow irritable in talking to the deaf and fail to realize how terribly they are shut out from the world. Hence, our school must teach them to rely upon themselves, to forget their handicap, and to try to be like other people, still realizing that they must work harder than normal people in order to make their way in the world. Courage and perseverance must be the motto of the deaf.

PHYSICAL CARE OF THE DEAF

This year the efficiency of the work in this line was increased through the kindness of Dr. Josephine E. Baker of the Board of Health, who allowed us to have a nurse to assist our aurist, Dr. George B. McAuliffe. The nurse comes every Thursday afternoon to help the doctor in the examination and treatment of eyes, ears and throat, and she also comes for half an hour every day to give special treatment to certain children, carrying out the doctor's directions. Besides our own children, Dr. McAuliffe has examined 20 children sent to us by other schools and by Miss Farrell's department. Some of these have been examined several times. Dr. McAuliffe again deserves our gratitude for his untiring efforts to help our children.

The report of Miss A. J. Smith, in charge of our physical training, tells of our progress and of our needs in this line.

REPORT ON PHYSICAL TRAINING

The plan of work for the physical training of the deaf constituted one of the most difficult problems presented to the Department of Physical Training. The plan of education in this day school for the deaf is in many ways materially different from that of other institutions for the deaf. It was necessary, therefore, to arrange an original course of study and special methods for teaching physical training in order to co-operate with the plan of work for this school.

The physical training is under the supervision of Dr. A. K. Aldinger and Miss Adela J. Smith of the Department of Physical Training. Five years of earnest work has resulted in an original system of physical training for the deaf, including many activities and methods of instruction attempted in no other institution for the deaf. It includes formal gymnastics, rhythmic exercises, mimetic exercises, games, team play, folk dancing, and this term training in swimming has been included. The plan co-operates with the regular class room work, the basis of which is speech reading and oral expression.

The majority of the deaf are inferior physically to the normal child, and much importance is attached, therefore, to their intelligent understanding of the value of systematic physical training and personal hygiene.

Through the formal gymnastics special attention has been given to the attainment of good posture. While this is important in the training of the normal child, it assumes greater significance in these handicapped children.

Special exercises are given to train alertness in response to commands and directions. These drills are given through speech reading. They are considered especially valuable in the training of deaf children since their alertness in comprehending a situation and acting upon it may often save them in times of danger on the crowded city streets. Through this training also the class teacher is aided in obtaining prompt attention of the class and the training of the pupils in control and inhibition power which necessarily is the foundation of the technical training of the deaf.

The series of rhythmic exercises and folk dances have helped very much in securing poise, posture and graceful carriage. The untrained deaf child has a characteristic shuffling gait, heavy carriage, and often an unbalanced and unsteady step. Much emphasis is, therefore, placed upon these rhythmic exercises, and for the younger children a series of exercises has been devised with ladders to educate a light step and erect carriage.

It is pleasing to note the cheerful effect folk dancing has had upon the girls. It has become a mode of expression and in its reaction has produced marked changes in the dispositions of the girls, who are apt to be stolid and expressionless or even morose. This year over fifty girls from this school took part in the fête at Central Park. Watching their happy faces it was difficult to realize that they differed in any way from the other girls all about them.

The boys' ambitions and ability in physical training are outgrowing the inadequate space of the school. Through the courtesy of the principal of P. S. 40 the instruction and the practice in basket-ball and athletics are conducted once a week in the large gymnasium of that school with much benefit and pleasure to the boys.

A new activity has been added to the course this term. During June the boys of the upper grades have received instruction in swimming. Two boys in this time qualified for the swimming button given by the P. S. A. L. It has been arranged for next term to give instruction and practice in swimming to the boys and the girls at the public swimming pool at the foot of East 23rd Street. The improvement in the health, strength and posture of these handicapped children can be readily appreciated in comparing them with the new pupils admitted during the year.

HYGIENIC SUGGESTIONS

There is need of better seating conditions. The seats in this school are old and cannot be properly adjusted because many of the adjustment tools cannot be supplied for this old furniture. The children in each grade vary in age and size in the same class room, since they are graded according to the speech training requirements of a grade. New adjustable desks are needed in order that adjustable plus and minus distance may be obtained. The seats should be a chair, like the new model Chandler seat and both desk and seat should be supplied with adjustment screws like those on the furniture for crippled children in order to save time in adjusting furniture.

The work in physical training requires better accommodations. The assembly room and playgrounds are now used for physical training and the class rooms also. The playgrounds are dark and poorly ventilated and without a ray of sunshine. The stables at the rear of the school make attempts at ventilation a farce. We want a large light airy gymnasium and shower baths; we want a big sunny roof playground for these children. We have demonstrated what can be accomplished even in small crowded quarters. It is of much importance that the deaf should have adequate accomodations for their physical welfare.

ADELA J. SMITH,
Department Physical Training—
Classes for Deaf, Blind, Crippled Children.

THE MENTAL SIDE

The school has been better graded this year and the introduction of a kindergarten has given a right start to the beginners. The class began with 10 children and has increased to 19. These children had absolutely no language. They had never spoken nor did they know that objects had names. Their sole means of communication were natural gestures. Owing to this, all kindergarten work had to be modified and adapted to these conditions. The greatest gain came through the occupations in that they gave the children the ability to care for themselves and to find something to do in the absence of the teacher. A beginning class of a dozen deaf children without this training would be impossible to handle.

Great effort has been made to improve the speech and speech reading. Children are encourage to try to read the lips of all visitors. Contests in speaking in the main room at the morning assembly have aroused the ambition of children, who never before had enough confidence to speak before an audience. One class of boys was so anxious to have their representative win that they spent their noontime coaching him on difficult sounds and proper phrasing and great was their joy when this boy won. These contests were limited to those classes which come to the morning assembly; but so great was the enthusiasm that a request came from all the classes down to the first year to be allowed to have a contest, a request which could not be denied.

Dramatization has been introduced and "Hansel and Gretel," as seen at the Century Theatre, was one of the ambitious performances of a 4B class. This work is difficult, as no child hears another, and all work is done by watching closely each other's lips, so as to know when to enter and to take part. The result is a greater alertness and a gain in facial expression so marked that visitors said, "They don't look like deaf children. Their faces are so expressive."

INDUSTRIAL WORK

This has made great strides this year. We have been surprised and gladdened at the willingness of business men to give our children an opportunity to work. We have an advantage in that we have but few children to place at a time. This gives us an opportunity to find what openings there are for the deaf and then we prepare the child for the position. In a letter from Mr. Charles R. Lamb, in which he urges a friend to accept one of our pupils, he speaks as follows: "I have one of the graduates with me, a young man, and find that apart from the personal equation as to ability the very handicap is in a sense an advantage in the designing room, as they are very quiet and concentrate on their work. All that is necessary is to give the required direction and they are faithful in carrying out their instructions."

The boys in the workshop have completed 201 articles, including library tables, desks, lamps and many small articles. They have also saved the Board about $150.00 in repairs they have done about the school.

The printing received such favorable comment that we were asked to take orders from outside. We had similar requests for our sewing, our shopwork and our industrial art. Upon our request, the Board granted us permission to be known as The Elementary and Trade School for the Deaf, which included permission to sell and take orders. This is a splendid opportunity for our pupils; but it adds to the difficulties of school administration, for we are trying to give these handicapped children the full elementary school education and at the same time we are giving them industrial training. We must be careful to give to each the proper proportion of time. This means hours and hours of planning, etc., so that the pupils may lose none of the academic work and yet get the industrial side. Our sessions are from nine till four, and cannot be continued longer because of the distances the children live from the school. In the institutions for the deaf the industrial work is done before nine, or in the late afternoon, or on Saturdays. This, of course, we cannot do, but it will probably be necessary in another year to start evening classes in craft and in speech work for former pupils who are working and for adults who may wish this aid. There may be need also of allowing graduates who can afford the time to return to the school, after graduation, for a year of craft work, to be given during the regular school hours.

THE GRADUATES

Five graduates left us in January and we have been much elated over the success of two of the boys. One a lad, totally deaf since he was six years old as a result of scarlet fever, entered Stuyvesant High School. This was the first attempt to try a deaf boy in a hearing high school. The blind boy has done splendid work in our high schools, but he hears all that is said. The deaf boy not only had to read the words from the different teachers' lips, but also the answers made by the pupils in the class. At first it was hard, hard work, but the boy was determined to succeed and at the close of this term he had no mark below 80 per cent. He has received no special consideration and no excuses were made for him, but he has had the kindness and sympathy of good teachers and of Dr. Von Nardroff. We feel this is a great success for the lad and for P. S. 47, where he attended school for five and a half years. The second boy has been deaf since he was two years old. He can hear loud sounds. He has entered the East Orange High School and has succeeded beyond our hopes.

In connection with this we must remember that the deaf acquire language through hard, hard work. Our vocabulary is largely the result of what we hear; the vocabulary of the deaf is a matter of memory to a great extent.

NEED OF A NEW BUILDING

Our field presents many problems most interesting and thought provoking and this school has an unusual opportunity to advance the work of the deaf. When we get a new building we can show its possibilities. At present our numbers increase, and our industrial department grows but the space does not increase. In each of three rooms two classes are being taught, which is difficult with deaf children. When the boys want to make a table or saw a large board they have to take their work out of the shop into a dark hole in order to have room. Worst of all, our pupils are here from nine till four and never have a chance to play outdoors because all the outdoors we have is a very small yard hemmed in by tall buildings. The new building ought to be large enough to house all our deaf children in one central well-graded school with a fine industrial equipment, in order to do justice to the work.

OUR SCHOOL PAPER

"The Voice" still continues to flourish and has received favorable mention as far as California. The contents and the workmanship are the children's own.

A YEAR'S PROGRESS

Looking over the year's work, we see a decided gain along all lines. Perhaps the greatest gains are the broadening of our industrial work, and the improvement in the dispositions and in the facial expressions of our pupils. When a handicapped child finds he is of use, his whole face brightens and becomes expressive.

One favor we beg, and this petition comes from the children themselves. Please omit the word "dumb" in speaking of this school. Every child is making earnest efforts to talk. It is hard to be called "deaf," but "dumb" somehow casts a stigma which is cruel, and which is not true of our pupils.

One of our most earnest desires is that the Board of Superintendents and the Board of Education may find time to visit the school to see if the expenditure of money and labor is justified in the results.

Respectfully submitted,

CARRIE WALLACE KEARNS.

Principal, Elementary and Trade School for the Deaf.

CLASSES FOR CRIPPLED CHILDREN

NEW YORK, July 15, 1914.

MR. WILLIAM H. MAXWELL,
  City Superintendent of Schools,

DEAR SIR:

The following table includes the schools having classes of crippled children, the number of classes in each school, and the register and average attendance in each school for the month of May, 1914.

	Public School	Classes	Register	Average Attendance
Manhattan	2P	11	167	158
"	27	3	47	45
"	30	1	18	17
"	44	2	43	35
"	67	5	84	65
"	68	3	61	54
"	70	1	19	16
"	104	1	20	19
"	107	3	75	57
		30	534	466
	14 (Tubercular Crippled)	1	16	16
The Bronx	8	1	26	22
"	44	1	21	19
"	47	1	12	11
		3	59	52
Brooklyn	64	1	33	24
"	80	1	16	14
"	162	4	82	68
"	168	1	26	23
		7	157	129

From this table it will be seen that there are at present 41 classes of crippled children with an attendance of 766 pupils.

During the past year the stages provided by the Board of Education have transported the children to each school named, except those children attending the annex to Public School 2, Manhattan.

Owing to the large expense involved and the desirability of appropriating more money for education in industrial lines, the Managers of the East Side Free School Association of Crippled Children have requested the Board of Education to pay $5,000 for rent of the building for crippled children and to defray one-half of the expense of transportation, $1,800, for the coming year. The Board of Superintendents recommended favorable action on this request. This building, which accomodates 11 classes and 167 pupils, is an ideal one for the purpose.

The Association for the Aid of Crippled Children, 5 Livingston Place, Stuyvesant Square, offered to aid the school authorities in caring for crippled children attending the public schools. The association expressed a willingness to assist in looking up crippled children not attending school, to report upon cases of absence, to visit the children at their homes, to look after their physical condition, to take them to hospitals and dispensaries, and to give relief or to obtain it through relief agency when advisable. This kind offer was accepted, and the City Superintendent sent a circular letter to the principals of all schools having classes of crippled children asking the principals to co-operate heartily with the association, to report cases that need attention, and to allow its representative to visit the classes as they desired.

There has been considerable agitation during the past year in favor of introducing much more industrial and vocational work into the classes for crippled children, and to make trade instruction prominent, but as yet the Board of Superintendents has not thought it advisable to recommend anything definite in this line.

If these children could be gathered into some one or two central buildings, the proposition would meet with greater favor.

The five classes in Public School 67, Manhattan, are to be transferred to Public School 69 at the opening of the coming term in order to provide additional rooms in Public School 67 for students in the High School of Commerce annex.

With the large number of crippled children attending the public schools, the need of medical attention in so many cases, much of it by specialists, it is my conviction that the time has come for the selection of a supervisor to take charge of this work. In addition to the need of medical attention, these children in most cases need suitable food, a special course of study that gives emphasis to physical and industrial training, and personal oversight by some competent person selected for the purpose.

Respectfully submitted,

ANDREW W. EDSON,
Associate City Superintendent.

REPORT ON VISITING TEACHERS

July 20, 1914.

Mr. William H. Maxwell,
   City Superintendent of Schools,

Dear Sir:

As per your request, I submit a brief account of the work of the visiting teachers for the term just closed.

For the past few years the Board of Education has requested the Board of Estimate to appropriate money for the employment of twenty-five visiting teachers, but no appropriation was made until last year, when money was granted for the employment of eight such teachers. Two of these were assigned to the Inspector of Ungraded Classes, four were appointed on February 1st to serve in two schools each, under the direction of district superintendents and principals. Two others have been appointed to begin service in September next.

The following persons were appointed as visiting teachers: Miss Margaret A. McGroarty, assigned to Public School 78 and Public School 159, Manhattan, James Lee, District Superintendent; Miss Cornelia L. Swinnerton, assigned to Public School 9 and Public School 43, The Bronx, John Dwyer, District Superintendent; Miss Alice B. Haines, assigned to Public School 5 and Public School 157, Brooklyn, John Griffin, District Superintendent; and Miss Katherine E. Manley, assigned to Public School 109, Boys, Public School 109, Girls, and Public School 165, Brooklyn, Charles W. Lyon, District Superintendent. The two appointed for service in September are Miss Christine Schaefer, to be assigned to Public School 2 and Public School 40, The Bronx, Joseph S. Taylor, District Superintendent, and Miss Jessie L. Louderback, to be assigned to Public School 19 and Public

School 104, Manhattan, Mrs. Ruth G. McGray, District Superintendent.

In order to systematize the work, special blanks were prepared for the visiting teachers to fill out and submit each day to the principal of the school, giving information in reference to each child whose case was investigated.

The following is a copy of the blank:

OFFICE OF THE CITY SUPERINTENDENT OF SCHOOLS

Special Report of Visiting Teacher

(To be submitted to the principal each day)
1. Name of child..
   Residence..
   School................Borough..........Grade......Age......
2. Special reasons for investigation.
3. Home and neighborhood conditions.
4. Attitude of parents towards the child and towards school.
5. Action taken by visitor and by parents.
6. Results.
7. Day and hour of visit.
   ...., 1914.
                    (Signed)..........................
                                        Visiting Teacher.

At the close of each week the visiting teacher was required to fill out a blank in duplicate to be sent to the district superintendent who forwarded a copy to the City Superintendent. This blank called for a statement of the number of visits to homes, the number of children looked after, the cause of the visit, remarks, and the hours of service each day.

At the close of the term a request was made of the visiting teachers, principals, and district superintendents for a brief statement of the general purpose and method of work of the visiting teachers; a comprehensive view of the several steps taken; a summary of the cases treated, with the reasons for the investigation, conditions found, and action taken; a list of the private agencies that have co-operated with the visiting teacher; the character of the assistance rendered; the conditions of the local neighborhood; the local school problems; significant cases illustrating the "human side" of the work, group activities organized through problems growing out of local needs, important conferences held or attended which tend to widen the influence of the visiting teachers, and suggestions for future betterment of the work.

A brief summary of the answers received from the visiting teachers is as follows:

GENERAL PURPOSE AND METHOD OF WORK

The general purpose of visiting teachers is to interest parents in school work and seek their co-operation; to raise the educational standard of the neighborhood; to obtain a better understanding between the school and the home; to discover, where possible, the causes and to deal with cases of irregular attendance, tardiness, misconduct, poor scholarship, nervousness, and ill health; and to advise parents or guardians in reference to the need of medical attention and where to secure it, and to suggest as to the need of proper food, clothing, open air, play and exercise.

The method followed is to report personally once or twice a week to the district superintendent, and daily to the principals of the schools to which she is assigned.

After securing the names and addresses of children in need of attention, the visiting teacher confers first with the children and class teachers, and consults the record blanks in order to secure as much information in advance as possible in reference to the children. By this course, the visiting teacher has a good school background that will enable her to talk with parents intelligently and helpfully. In some cases the assistance of charitable or social agencies is at once invoked. After these interviews the visiting teacher reports back to the principal of the school as to the steps taken, to advise farther in reference to these cases and to secure the names of other children in need of attention. Many of these cases need several visits.

SUMMARY OF THE CASES TREATED

Miss McGroarty: Number of visits, 403; number of cases treated, 312.

Miss Swinnerton: Number of cases treated, 81.

Miss Haines: Number of cases treated, 372.

Miss Manley: Number of cases treated, 434; Number of visits, 967.

CONDITIONS INVESTIGATED

Irregular attendance caused by illness and lack of interest; lateness; misconduct; poor scholarship; a conviction that the parents were more at fault than the children; bad environment.

CONDITIONS FOUND

Children incorrigible at home; bad companions and bad environment; on the street late at night; immorality; adverse home conditions; lack of parental authority; sickness in the family; children kept out of school to help care for younger members of the family; both parents at work away from home; illiteracy of parents and indifference as to an education; slothful and indifferent mothers; waywardness of children without knowledge of parents; extreme povery; and foreign-born girls over fourteen years of age striving to evade the law requiring them to secure an employment certificate.

ACTION TAKEN

Parents instructed as to the necessity of an education for their children; mothers induced to take an interest in the mental and moral development of their children; group conferences with parents at school; cases of chronic truancy referred to the truant officers; application made to the Bureau of Charities, Labor Bureau, the Gerry Society, the Salvation Army, local settlements, hospitals and dispensaries, and private agencies, for material assistance; and children induced to take a right attitude towards the school.

OUTCOME OF INVESTIGATION

In most of the cases of irregular attendance the delinquent children returned to school after one visit by the visiting teacher; interest taken in these exceptional cases by individuals and by societies; children cared for by "big brothers" or "big sisters"; employment secured for parents out of work; better food, better clothing, and medical treatment secured for those in need; arrangements made to have young children sent to a day nursery so that the older children may attend school; increased interest by parents in the children and in all agencies for the betterment of their children.

AGENCIES THAT CO-OPERATED WITH THE VISITING TEACHERS

Society for the Prevention of Cruelty to Children, Silver Cross Day Nursery, Children's Aid Society, Hebrew Sisterhood, Board of Health Clinics, Public Education Society, Child Labor Association, Charity Organization Society, Association for Improving the Condition of the Poor, United Neighborhood Guild, St. Ann's Parish House, Maxwell House, Supervisor of School Nurses, Social Service Exchange, Social Service Department of Hospitals, The Bronx House, College Settlement, University Settlement, Greenwich House, Supervisor of Department of Health T. B. Clinic, Russell Sage Foundation, New York State Charities Conference, Conferences of Volunteer Workers, Hebrew Aid Society, Bureau of Charities, the Gerry Society, the Salvation Army, Willoughby Settlement, Eagle Information Bureau, United Neighborhood Guild, the local hospitals and churches.

A FEW SIGNIFICANT CASES

"A volunteer worker was induced by the visiting teacher to take an interest in a delinquent girl of fifteen who needed constant oversight, to introduce her to a Domestic Arts Club and to keep up an acquaintance with her at home."

"A boy whose conduct was bad and attendance poor, was found to be living with a step-mother whom he disliked. The boy was taken to another relative by the father, with good results in attendance and conduct."

"A boy nine years of age in the ungraded class was a source of annoyance to his teacher and the members of his class because of a bad habit, due to certain physical conditions, which could be removed by an operation. The parents' consent was secured to have the operation performed and all arrangements were made for his admission to the hospital. The operation was successful and the habit was corrected."

"Two colored boys were reported because of irregular attendance. In visiting the home the mother was found to be sick in bed and the father with work only about three days a week. They were behind in rent and had pawned most of their clothes and furniture to buy food. The mother was not receiving medical attention. The boys came to school without food. As immediate relief from the charity organizations could not be obtained, some of the teachers and the visiting teacher provided food for the family, clothes for the boys, and medical treatment for the mother. One of the societies of the colored church became interested in the family and temporary aid was given."

"A girl transferred from another school was reported as being a habitual truant. The child's home was found to be far below the standard and the child was kept at home to do the mother's work as janitress. The father, a consumptive, was away from home and the mother was indifferent as to the welfare of the child, who lacked clothing and proper attention. Clothing was provided and the child's attendance improved. On a later visit, a boy about ten years of age, who had never been to school, was discovered. Arrangements were at once made for his admission to school."

TESTIMONY OF PRINCIPALS

"Much of the work accomplished this year could not have been done without our visiting teacher. We have individual cases enough to date to warrant paying her salary for the next twenty years. When a young girl of fifteen is saved from a life of shame, and put where she will lead a self-respecting, upright life, the value is far beyond anything that money can express, as was done in several instances."

"The 'human side' would not be sufficiently exemplified were I to omit mention of securing work for fathers and mothers out of employment. After all when the bread and butter need cries out, it cannot be satisfied with philosophy, pure and simple. Our work is too young to have given time to develop group activities or organizations. In fact the individual work was so effective that our entire neighborhood shows its influence."

"It seems to me that there is not as yet the proper co-ordination between the work of the nurse, the truant officer, and the visiting teacher. Each one has a distinct field but still over-lapping. The truant officer seeks to return the absent child, but his district is so large that there must be short time given somewhere, and I think there ought to be time given to bringing in the children who play openly in the streets. Intricate cases that require special treatment might be turned over to the visiting teacher. She in turn should be able to hand over to the school nurse the cases requiring hospital or similar treatment. So the nurse, when she finds improper home environment, should call in the good offices of the visiting teacher. Some such system of interdependence would finally improve all the work."

"It is next to impossible to convince some of the parents of this section that the law has any right to interfere with them in deciding what they shall do with their children. They resent any interference, and seem to think that it is not in keeping with the liberty that they expected to find in this country.

"Frequent conferences were held with the visiting teacher for the purpose of deciding what steps were to be taken in individual cases, suggestions were made as to method of procedure, and in general effort was made to co-operate with the visiting teacher in such manner as to impress the parents with the fact that her work was in harmony with the work of the school, and that the only purpose of both was to contribute to the welfare of the children, so that they might grow up to be good men and good women.

"I wish to take this opportunity to testifying to the earnestness, sincerity, and industry which have characterized the work of the visiting teacher. She has succeeded in gaining the confidence of the parents, and I am satisfied that her influence for good will be greatly increased in the future."

"The early attempts to bring the home and the school into closer relation were not altogether successful because they relied too greatly upon the efforts of the teacher and of the supervisor, after the regular school hours, to establish this delicate adjustment, oblivious of the fact that this duty required the display of powers undimmed by fatigue and unclouded by anxiety. It also became evident that the establishment of harmonious relations between the teacher and parent demanded special powers and ability, which every teacher did not possess; again, conditions frequently made it necessary for the visit to be made in the evening, when the father had returned home from his work, all of which added to the complexity of the problem. These difficulties called into existence a new agency for establishing permanent and efficient relations between teacher and parent, to short-circuit, so to speak, the school and the home,—and the visiting teacher stepped in to make the connection.

"To enumerate all the specific duties of the visiting teachers is impossible. Each of the factors of the problem—the home, the parents, the school, and the pupil, separately and in combination, presents constantly changing needs. The home presents problems of povery and of destitution, of domestic unhappiness and of parental neglect, which the visiting teacher must seek to study and to solve. The parents require advice how to procure employment and instruction how to help their children overcome the influences of an unfavorable environment; they must be stimulated to persevere and inspired to consider the welfare of their children their chief concern. The child must be studied to determine the particular causes which are hampering his development. The organization and management of the school must be scrutinized to correct any defects of maladjustment, which may cause friction and retard the pupil's progress. Splendid indeed must be the mental and personal endowments of the individual who can accomplish all this and who can bring to bear upon this work powers of insight, inspiration, sympathy, tact, common sense and indefatigable industry. I am very glad to state that our visiting teacher fully measures up to the high requirements of her position.

"In performing her duties, the visiting teacher naturally avails herself of all the agencies whose co-operation is helpful. She has enlisted the help of philanthropic individuals and the services of the Hebrew Educational Society for recreational opportunities, the clinics and hospitals in the neighborhood of the school, the Hebrew Aid Society for the relief of poverty, the Social Service Society, the Bureau of Charities and the Children's Aid Society."

"This work is conducted in probably one of the poorest sections of our City. The ignorance of many of the parents of our language and our institutions, the frequent and protracted periods of industrial depression, the congestion of the population—all combine to make the "bread" problem the one of all absorbing interest, and to thrust upon outside agencies, to a large extent, the training of the younger generation. All the visiting teachers' cases illustrate the need of a mediatorial office between the home and the school."

"May I, in closing, express the hope that this splendid social service may escape the ever besetting danger of being judged largely by elaborate statistical records rather than by the spiritual results achieved, which cannot readily manifest themselves in reports? I believe that the present plan, which allows of perfect freedom of action in the interest of the children, should be retained, in order that there may be no danger of confusing the formal letter of a written report which killeth and the spirit of service which giveth life."

"Our chief problem is to make the parents understand their responsibility. They do not understand English. They do not readily adjust themselves to new conditions in this country, and they do want the school to shoulder all their responsibilities. They cannot and do not exact obedience from their children, and the children have no respect for their parents."

Pupils sign their own report cards, or tell their parents that cards are only given below the 7th year, that pupils who stay a second term in a class must be promoted at the end of that term whether he works or not. The parent naturally thinks that the child is always right, and it is most difficult to convince him that we cannot always please the child. The parents expect us to do favors for them. The cause of all this disobedience, untruthfulness and disrespect lies with the parent who, instead of firmly and kindly insisting upon a child doing the right thing, bribes him to do it. In school we have no trouble along these lines, but these conditions do not prevail in the home."

"Our visiting teacher has been untiring in her efforts to bring about a proper adjustment of school and home. She is most faithful in her work and very tactful in interviews with parents, and most willing to act upon any suggestion that will help in the work."

"I believe that the visiting teacher can and does accomplish a great deal of good inasmuch as she brings about a closer co-operation between the school and the home. I do not know that I can offer any suggestions for future betterment of her work, except that I belive her usefulness would be much greater than it is if the various relief organizations co-operated with her more readily and easily. Although I believe that the roots of most of our problems are too deep to be reached by our relief organizations, still many maladjustments, mental and physical, can be corrected to some degree by these organizations."

TESTIMONY OF DISTRICT SUPERINTENDENTS

"The visiting teacher is a woman of much tact and her experience as a nurse under the Board of Health has been of very great value. She has spent her own money to procure food, shoes, and clothing for children, and she visits homes at night and goes to distant parts of the city to consult with fathers at their places of business."

"I have great pleasure in certifying to the efficiency and zeal of the lady and have no doubt that in the future her influence will be increasing and helpful."

"In my opinion the work that should be assigned to the visiting teacher is that of the special cases that could not be very well assigned to the class teacher, the nurse, or the truant officer. The fact is that teachers are altogether too busy to make a careful diagnosis of the important cases in their classes. Our visiting teacher has had a few cases requiring attention to which no teacher would possibly have time enough to give."

"One of the benefits of the work of the visiting teacher is that the class teachers are likely to take more pains in diagnosing the cases of wayward pupils. One of my principals informs me that already his teachers are more interested in these social conditions than they were before the visiting teacher commenced work."

With the work so well begun, with the testimony of all in immediate charge of the visiting teachers so uniformly and strongly in favor of the retention and extension of the work, I strongly urge an appropriation for the employment of twenty-five visiting teachers for the coming year.

Respectfully submitted,

ANDREW W. EDSON,

Chairman, Committee on Elementary Schools.

CPSIA information can be obtained
at www.ICGtesting.com
Printed in the USA
BVHW091827261118
534029BV00017B/530/P